T0113711

UNIVERSAL SPIRITUAL LAWS
and
HEALING

OTHER BOOKS/JOURNAL BY
RONALD L. COLE, M.D.

"The Gentle Greeting"

Planning a Family Oriented loving and
Spiritual Pregnancy and Birth

"Prenatal Psychology 100 Year"

(Authored by Experts in Prenatal Psychology)

Chapter 14- Spiritual Aspects of Birth and a Physician's Evolvement

"Pre-Perinatal Psychology Journal, 9(3), Spring 1995"

An Enlightened Obstetrician's Dilemma:
Combining Medical and Spiritual Understanding

UNIVERSAL SPIRITUAL LAWS and HEALING

Unbreakable God Given Laws
That Created and Govern
The Universe and Guide You
To Create a Loving, Healthy
Life and World

RONALD L. COLE, M.D.

BALBOA.PRESS
A DIVISION OF HAY HOUSE

Balboa Press books may be ordered through booksellers or by contacting:

Balboa Press
A Division of Hay House
1663 Liberty Drive
Bloomington, IN 47403
www.balboapress.com
844-682-1282

Print information available on the last page.

ISBN: 978-1-9822-4911-3 (sc)
ISBN: 978-1-9822-4912-0 (e)

Library of Congress Control Number: 2020911037

Balboa Press rev. date: 08/27/2020

CONTENTS

ACKNOWLEDGEMENTS

Initial collection of knowledge for this book began back in 1994. During my many years of spiritual research, study and application, which started around 1966, I have worked with many teachers and supporters. I would like to acknowledge and thank the major one's that contributed to this book. I would first like to thank my very special and caring wife, Karen, for the many long hours it took to type the manuscript and to tolerate my editing efforts. I would also like to thank one of my sons, Kevin, who offered to help with the promotion of the book once it is published.

I would like to acknowledge Rev. Beverly Burdick-Carey who was Sanctioned by the National Spiritualist Association of Churches, and was a teacher, licensed healer, spiritual councilor and certified medium. We shared about 20 years working together as my teacher, medium and channel who brought Quan Yin into my life as the source of highly evolved and valuable spiritual truths that were recorded on approximately 600 audio tapes. A number of these tapes formed the bases for this book. Quan Yin is well documented in many books as a Goddess of Compassion, Mercy and Motherhood in Eastern countries.

Over the past years I have worked with many other evolved people that are too numerous to count, but I sincerely thank them. Finally, I want to acknowledge you the reader who will hopefully evolve spiritually by using these Universal Spiritual Laws. These laws can bring the real truth to this world so we can all live much higher evolved lives with minimal disease and negativity.

INTRODUCTION

Universal Spiritual Laws

In our world today there is an uncountable number of laws, rules and regulations that govern every aspect of our daily activity and existence. They occur at every level of society starting at the family level and moving up through neighborhood, city, and state, nation and the entire world organizations. These rules and laws are mainly a collection of individual man's and societies' opinions on how you should behave and order every aspect of your life. Of course these laws vary greatly depending upon which society, organizations, political party or country of which you are a member. So, what is accepted or expected belief or behavior in one grouping of people may be greatly destined or punishable in another group. This is similar to the "fact" that in this world we have hundreds of "one true religions". How could that be with such a vast difference of beliefs, that each claim they are the only "true religion" of the only "True God"? Why, because each one is based on some person's beliefs and opinions that first started the movement group, or religion. Also, often the original thinking or basis either gets lost in antiquity or undergoes many reinterpretations over many generations. These revisions are then based on the beliefs of the current "ruling faction" which often is motivated by desire to gain or remain in control and get people to act or "behave" in a manner that benefits those in control. Also the man-made laws are usually accompanied by a list of punishments that will result from not following the established beliefs or laws such as, loss of privileges, fines, prison or eternal punishment.

Universal Spiritual Laws are completely different from the above.

First, they are not man-made laws. Secondly, they do not change or get reinterpreted by any current ruling class. Third, they are not based on repentant and punishable principles that may apply more to one group or individual than another. Fourth, and very uniquely, the Universal Spiritual Laws cannot be broken. You are governed by them no matter what you think, say or do. You will be affected by them in either a positive way and speed up your evolution or in a negative way and slow down your evolution depending on whether your thoughts, words or deeds are positive or negative. It is your choice. Obviously the lessons are much easier if the laws are used in a positive way. Unlike man-made laws, in which if you don't get caught or discovered you won't be subjected to the punishment. Universal Spiritual Laws will affect you whether or not you are "caught". Nothing is hidden from the Oneness of the Universe. The laws are always in effect and will not go away.

Universal Spiritual Law wasn't created, it creates. The physical and nonphysical realms were created by Universal Spiritual Law. Universal Spiritual Law has always existed. Universal Spiritual Law, just like God, has no beginning or end, it simply is.

Since they are not man-made they contain no ego, no self-serving basis, they do not vary from society to society or time to time and they are not arbitrary. Universal Spiritual Laws are divine laws of God. They are immutable and do not change themselves, but they permit the Essence of God or Creation to be mutable, growing and evolving. Also very importantly, Universal Spiritual Laws are based on the highest and most purest of energy which is unconditional love. Therefore, they are totally impersonal, impartial and apply to everyone and everything equally. Therefore, this leads us to the obvious importance of this book, which is knowing, understanding, and the positive and loving application of Universal Spiritual Laws.

That is to speed up our spiritual evolution/growth and makes our life more joyful, rewarding, abundant and loving.

It would obviously be of great benefit to us to know the "rules of the game of life." By knowing the rules to "play by" you can take responsibility for yourself and be in control of your life and point it in the direction you choose. Unfortunately, for many people, that doesn't leave God or anyone else to blame the seemingly undesirable aspects of their life on. That will require a major attitude adjustment for society, but it will bring positive results and changes that only you can make. Keep a very important fact in mind. THAT EACH OF LIFE'S EXPERIENCES PRESENTS AN OPPORTUNITY TO LEARN A LESSON AND PROGRESS IN ONE'S GROWTH PATTERN. The quicker you learn a lesson the sooner you will not have to repeat it.

There is only one primary Universal Spiritual Law, the most important law and the law from which other laws are derived. It is the Law of Love. All Universal Spiritual laws are intimately intertwined with each other as well as the common thread of love. This book will cover the major laws that are derived from the primary law, as well as the primary law itself.

During my approximately fifty years of intense personal study and application of spiritual truths, as a physician I eventually realized that spiritual truths were the real key to healing. These truths and the Universal Spiritual Laws are healing in action. Along with the Universal Spiritual Laws I also asked for insights to the healing aspect of each law. If all Universal Spiritual Laws were consciously followed in a positive, loving way by all individuals, illness and disease would simply disappear along with all other negative aspect of life such as war, crime, hatred, fear and all domestic discomfort. All could be healed.

My understanding of healing evolved as, I combined my medical and spiritual understanding. I had the perfect situation to do this- my medical practice as a obstetrician and gynecologist, which allowed me to start at the beginning of life as one would enter this world. Some of my research was published in the Pre-and Perinatal Psychology Journal,9 (3),Spring 1995 entitled, "An Enlightened Obstetrician's Dilemma: Combining Medical and Spiritual Understandings." I also presented it at the Prenatal Psychology International Conventions in Washington, D.C. and San Francisco. I would like to briefly give you insights to what I have learned.

Truth of Healing

Most people, particularly in the Western World, believe the true causes of healing are pharmaceuticals, surgery, numerous medical treatment modalities, physicians and other medical personal. Instead of being the true cause of the healing, these are the "mechanics" of healing. The true cause that allows the healing to occur is the thinking and beliefs of the patient themselves. It is probably a little strange hearing a long experienced physician say that, but I've learned it to be true. I'm sorry to say physicians do not heal people, they actually help people heal themselves. If a patient subconsciously does not want to be healed, they will not be healed.

Why would anyone choose to create an illness or disease or not be healed? Because of guilt, fear, anger or any other subconscious type of negative beliefs or thinking. It is all done on a subconscious level that we are not aware of.

Fairly early in my spiritual research I was introduced to a technique called channeling that provides truthful spiritual insights to people's subconscious reasoning and actions. As we are told, "Knock and the door will be opened." I was led to a highly evolved, loving and gifted medium named Reverend Beverly Burdick-Carey. Reverend Burdick-Carey brought in/channeled a well-known historical highly evolved spiritual entity named Quan Yin. Her teachings were based on unconditional love and pure truth from the high spiritual realms, therefore avoiding human ego, and desire for power and control. A twenty plus year working and learning relationship with both followed during which I received logical and accurate insights as to why things happen in lives both positive and negative. What consciously makes no seemingly logical sense "on the surface," makes perfect sense when gained subconscious insights are added to the life and medical understandings and circumstances. I have hundreds of individual situations recorded giving examples of the true reasons why people created situations in their life of a negative nature.

Understanding Universal Spiritual Laws and their applications helps you change negative beliefs and thinking into positive and loving ones, which create a healing atmosphere. This illustrates the very close relationship between Universal Spiritual Laws and the true healing process. Healing applies to all aspects of our life, and not just illness and disease.

When your health or other life situations are not normal, do not wonder why God put it in your life, or someone else caused it to happen. Look within yourself for insights as to changing your thinking guided by these laws. I was told by my teacher that "all disease is a reflection of internal dys-ease" and I have found this to be true.

In conclusion, I want to make a very important point to you about healing. As a physician, I always followed the standard medical guidelines we were taught in medical school and residency first and foremost. That is obviously required to practice medicine in today's profession. When I could use my spiritual insights to help my patient,

I would do so. The major point is that you yourself can apply Universal Spiritual Laws to the accepted practice of medicine and take back control of your health and healing as well as take advantage of all the benefits that medical practice provides.

Healing Example

To help you understand how healing truly works I will share a great learning example I got from a patient of mine. A relatively young patient of mine who had previously had a hysterectomy came into my office with the complaint of severe pelvic pain that lasted for more than two weeks each time she had intercourse. As I started taking a careful history, she indicated some time back she had gone to her family physician. After a short history and a pelvic exam, he abruptly told her, she had a vaginal yeast infection and an incurable sexually transmitted disease called herpes and sent her home. Not long after the visit the severe symptoms started.

This occurred at the early social understanding of herpes as a venereal disease. Also her family physician was an older physician who didn't spend much time with each patient and was rather gruff in his bedside manners. I'm not sure how he diagnosed the herpes.

When I examined this patient her pelvic exam revealed no abnormal findings. She also seemed very "down" and self-conscious about what he had told her and he gave her no education or insights about his findings.

My conclusion at the time was rather clear after talking to, listening to and examining her, two factors, first: the way her family physician talked to her and secondly: her limited understanding of herpes and her resulting negative reasoning and thinking about her situation mainly involving guilt. It was apparent to me that she felt guilty about being told she had a venereal disease she didn't understand and she needed to be punished for this. So in her subconscious mind, the best way for the "punishment to fit the crime" was to have severe pain after intercourse. If you truly believe it, your mind can create it.

Realizing this, I spent quite a bit of time educating her about how common herpes was and it was something she could have contracted years ago and not just promiscuous people get it. As I talked to her I could see her "letting go" of the guilt and her self-image was rapidly improving. The joy seemed to be returning to her. The treatment I recommended to her would never be found in a medical text book and indeed it was very unconventional, but here it is. Armed with her new and positive thinking and education, I told her to stop on her way home and get a bottle of her favorite wine and go home and seduce her husband. About a month or more later, I thought about her and wondered how she was doing. So I told my office manager to call her and ask her to come in for a visit and that I would not charge her for the visit. I wanted to complete my education on her case.

When she came into the office, I asked her two important questions. First question I asked her was: "How was she doing?" Her answer was, "Great". Second question was: "How is your sex life?" Her answer was simply, "Couldn't be better!" I realized she taught me more than I taught her. So I didn't cure her of anything, I simply helped her cure herself.

One general comment I will say that also presents a similar example, are the countless number of surgeries I have done over forty years, where there was no abnormal physical findings to explain the patients severe symptoms. Yet, the symptoms were gone following the patients recovery. The power of the human mind is unlimited. So I ask you to keep these points and this example in mind as we discuss healing throughout this book.

UNIVERSAL SPIRITUAL LAW OF LOVE

The primary Universal Spiritual Law, the Law of Love, states that every aspect of the consciousness of God and Creation loves itself and every other aspect of the consciousness of God unconditionally.

In simple terms, the great immutable Universal Primary Law of Love means that all of God, is and ever shall be unconditional love. Unconditional, a love that asks nothing in return, is without human emotion, is without judgement, and is without expectation. It does not ask or expect to be loved in return. It does not judge its own quality or any other quality of love. It has no needs to be met, it is absolute peace and harmony. It exists in and of itself in perfection and as such is a guiding light to all lesser love. Unconditional love is only capable of being unconditional love. In its state of perfection it transmutes all things into unconditional love. Because it expects nothing and judges not, the only thing it is capable of being or doing is love, and creating more love. It has no goal, no ambition, and no desire. Unconditional love exists as immutable, which can never be other than loving and it has no needs, desires, ambitions or expectations.

So important is the Law of Love, that if a person or any life form can act in accordance with it, then it is automatically in accordance with every other Universal Spiritual Law. Love is the true essence of God. At this time in evolution, no human being absolutely understands and operates in the full range of the Law of Love. But it is possible for one to experience unconditional love without totally understanding what it is or what they are doing.

The human emotions of need, expectations and desires are particularly important when you are working towards gaining unconditional love in interpersonal relationships. It is often easier to unconditionally love a being with whom you have very little actual physical connection. There is no urge to desire or expect, or have ambition where a stranger is concerned. Where the Law of Love is often broken is within families and close friend situations.

As an example: lovers, when they choose to share their life, they always have expectations of the relationship, of things that they will receive together, of what they expect of themselves in the relationship and what they expect of their partner in the relationship. Because these expectations are human in nature they automatically make it very difficult for mates to achieve unconditional love towards one another.

One major expectation in today's human and social relationships is that of fidelity. In general, societies' belief in fidelity demands that in a relationship the two people only love another. One must realize that there is physical or sexual love and spiritual love, which is obviously far more all-encompassing. So individuals do not have to make physical love to feel love for each other. Physical love is only a very small aspect of true or unconditional love. We as humans, love many things including pets, hobbies, wonders' of nature, friends and activities that don't involve physical love or sex. God's Law of Love has no limitations, it is simple. All should love all. It is natural for all to love all, for All is God and God is All.

Additionally, spouses expect from one another, cooperation, understanding, certain duties to be performed by each mate in a mated pair. All of these things are in opposition to the Law of Love.

As humans grow and evolve, they will cease to place limitations upon their abilities to love. The reason for the limitation is fear, and fear is one of the greatest impediments to unconditional love. Humans fear that if they do not make laws, conditions, or agreements that will bind them to one another they will lose the object of their love, and thus they have done so for thousands of centuries upon the earth. They have made laws governing love and most of them not in harmony with God's Law of Love.

Another area in which it is easy to see how the Universal Law of Love is not observed is in parental love for their children, be it blood parents, stepparents, foster parents, and adoptive parents. Most parents unconditionally love the newly born infant, but soon this love becomes adulterated by expectations, by hopes, desires and ambitions for the child. All parents say lovingly, I do not care what my child does as long as he or she is happy, but that in itself places a condition. It is not necessary to want happiness for a child, it is human, and to humans it is natural. If humans understood the Law of Love, they would know that happiness is a natural part of love, and if all were operating within the Law of Love, all would be happy. Therefore, the parent is expressing desire and expectations for the child, when in fact, the parent has no way of helping that expectation become reality, unless they are working within the Universal Law of Love.

Parents believe that they are unselfish in loving if they do not interfere in their child's life, but only wish for the child be happy. It is not necessary for parents to wish happiness for the child, let it decide for itself whether it will be happy or unhappy. In family relationships, in almost every possible way the Universal Law of Love is adulterated in the name of love. It is human possessiveness, not unconditional love, and humanity as a whole is not yet ready to understand these things. The idea that expectations of faithful devotion to duty, is not according to God's Law of Love, most people on the earth today would not find that they can accept this. They have been taught conditions through many generations to believe that love means expectations, ambitions, the desire to please one another and to surrender to one another. When, indeed love means merging. When two people truly merge their consciousness they seek to avoid the alterations of love. Their sense of absolute oneness enables them to love unconditionally. Few, indeed experience this total merging with other beings. Those who do in society today would probably be considered rather rare or different. Their way of expressing their love for one another would not be as most humans understand it.

Humans are growing and will come to this realization that possessiveness is not love, ambition is not love, expectation is not love, jealousy is not love and fear is not love. As you are learning these things do not attempt to change too rapidly or too radically. Allow others to at least keep up with you in your understanding and expression of love. There would be little profit in saying to your children for instance, that you have no ambitions for them, no expectations for them, that you love them exactly as they are and whatever they do is acceptable to you. In the society that we live in this would not be a practical thing to do at this time. Parental loving guidance can merge and evolve and must in our current society.

While it is important that every individual grow spiritually, individuals must keep in mind they have chosen to be upon the earth plane in a human form. So they must, to some degree, follow the human customs that are necessary to maintain order in society until unconditional love is understood and practiced by all members of society, otherwise children would feel that you did not love them.

These are the hardest things, the most difficult things that stand in the way of understanding and living in accordance with the primary

Law of Love. Divine love is so very different from human love that to most, it is at this point incomprehensible. Many people often talk about unconditional love and many even feel that they express it, but few if any are evolved enough to truly understand unconditional love is our highest goal.

Perhaps the closest examples of unconditional love upon earth today are between humans and other animal species or domestic pets, such as canines, felines and other warm blooded and furry beings. Whatever humans take into their homes and hearts, they seem more capable of giving unconditional love to, rather than to other human beings. This is due in part to the human belief that they are the most intelligent species upon the planet, the only reasoning species, and the only species that understands itself and has self-realization. Humans are incorrect in all of these beliefs of course but they continue to believe them. Because of this, they are capable of loving other life forms that they have taken into their homes without expectation, without ambition and without desire. Therefore, the affection is given, the care is given, the love is given, and if the animal companion in some ways seems to show that it is returning the love, this causes great joy.

On the other hand, some of our animal friends exhibit unconditional love to humans. As an example you can take a dog and put it with the meanest most loathing, as far as human customs goes, rapist, murderer and it would probably do the same things with that person that it would do with a very caring, loving person, assuming the person didn't beat it and abuse it. If the dog bites the owner then supposedly that unconditional love on the part of the human probably will rapidly change to very conditional love, because the supposedly non-intelligent, non-reasoning member of the family, the pet, has exhibited a personality and desired pattern of its own.

It may well be in conflict with the desired pattern of its own. It may well be in conflict with the desired pattern with the rest of the family, and therefore conditions now exist. When conditions exist it is no longer unconditional love, it becomes human love, which is far from unconditional love.

These things are not to say that human love is wrong, of course it is not wrong, it is part of the journey. Humans loving their infants, loving their mates, loving their animal companions, shows that they are capable of unconditional love, and this is very encouraging.

Let us talk of some of the ways in which unconditional love can be achieved. It can be one step at a time. Remember that you are only responsible for your feelings, actions, motivations, etc. You are responsible for creating unconditional love for yourself and not all other aspects of God. You have no responsibility where the other aspects are concerned. It is not up to you to create unconditional love in them. They have that responsibility. It is a fact of human nature that some level of unconditional love is more easily achieved when you are not in constant physical contact with an individual. For instance, humans are more capable of loving somewhat unconditionally, people that they have never seen, people they feel a sense of concern or sorrow for, and they pray in a totally uninvolved and unconditional way for that individual. We find also many times in a relationship that there has been trouble between two individuals, that when they are no longer in a face to face situation, it becomes possible to love more unconditionally. The secret is impersonal love. You can more easily love impersonally someone you either, no longer see or have never seen. It is harder to love impersonally, your spouse, your children, your co-workers, for these are people with whom you interact in a very personal way, and you do and say things that irritate one another. We practice learning and observing unconditional love by, for instance, choosing a group of people that we do not know, and sending that group unconditional love.

You may pick a person or group known to not be very lovable. They may stand accused and in many cases convicted of great atrocities towards other beings. They are not a lovable group of people, according to human conscience, but what better individual or group to practice the art of unconditional love. How do you begin this? By directing prayers to them, only prayers, do not pray for any specific things, do not pray that they give up their wicked ways, for that is an expectation. Do not put any conditions. Simply two or three times daily quietly close your mind to outside interference, and project the idea of love to them, just love, simply put, "I send you love, I send you love, I send you love."

You are not asking anything of them in return, you are not expecting anything of them, you are making them a free gift of your love for them. To succeed in such an endeavor will greatly increase your understanding of and participation in God's divine, immutable and Universal Law of Love. If you find that your prayer becomes tainted with the idea that you hope, if you love them enough they will change, stop the prayer and start all over again, so that your mind is only in tune with the thought, I send you love.

This will be a mighty step forward if you can accomplish it. If you accomplish total impersonal and some level of unconditional love, that group or individual will know it when it happens. This does not mean that they will change, it means that you have come into a state of unconditional love towards all groups of entities that seem so difficult to love.

There is one very important aspect of the Universal Law of Love, the greatest thing of all is no expectations, no desire, no ambitions, and you must remember that all those things are part of unconditional love. But by the Law of Attraction, one of the secondary laws, it is so ordained that whatever is sent out must return and unconditional love sent out must return unconditional love to the sender. Not always does that unconditional love come to the individual or individuals to whom it has been directed, but in some way one who honestly sends unconditional love, participates in unconditional love, begins to understand unconditional love and receives unconditional love.

So we capsulize the whole thing by saying simply, "Unconditional love means that you desire nothing in return, that your love goes freely without conditions, without expectations, without ambition or desire, and is returned to you in exactly the same way". If you think, I will unconditionally love, so that I may receive unconditional love, you have, of course, altered the whole process.

In truth, in being at One with God, it is just as important to unconditionally love yourself as to unconditionally love other life forms or beings. Many people have difficulty loving themselves. Probably one of the main reasons why, is that they feel everyone else should come before them. This is not an absolute rule and one cannot serve others, help others and truly love others until they learn to love and help themselves. Lack of self-worth, self-confidence and self-imposed guilt causes many people to behave in ways that are very unbecoming and detrimental to their spiritual growth and social image. Unfortunately, many organizations, religions and groups strongly teach that you should always put others before yourself. This lessens your ability to express and feel love.

When one feels jealous, inferior, guilt, sinful and useless, they cannot project much love, particularly unconditional love. One can project love much better from an attitude of loving one's self. So all should be taught and learn the importance of self-love. One can certainly love themselves at the same time they love others. There is

NO limit on the amount of love one can feel and project. There is an unlimited supply of love that we all possess. We just need to realize that and start actively reflecting that love.

Love, you see, has many components, one of which is education or teaching. As a loving parent will chastise an erring child, so the immutable Law of Love permits us to learn by making what we call mistakes. Love does not interfere with our education, it augments it. Unconditional love does not smother us with protective fear, unconditional love frees us to make our own choices. Unconditional love expects nothing, therefore is incapable of making demands. Unconditional love is not a wild emotion, it is a gentle state of being, asking nothing, giving all, accepting all, rejecting nothing, permitting all things and interfering in nothing. Unconditional love binds all things together, for it is the very essence of God. At the same time unconditional love is the only power that has the capacity to simply, by its being, transmute anything into itself. It does not force, it absorbs. It does not command change, it transmutes.

Without the power and energy of love, nothing could exist, and yet unconditional love asks nothing in return. By the very power of demanding nothing and accepting all love is the only real power, and in time there will be only love, all other Universal Laws will have fulfilled their purpose, which is quite simply to create love.

Remember that Universal Spiritual Laws apply to all life forms, but we as humans quite often think of ourselves as the only true or important life form. Contrary to the majority of societies thinking and the very fragile human ego, that "holier-than-thou" concept just isn't true in the broadest or spiritual sense. If we are all part of the Oneness of God, then who has the right to say that any part is more important than another. The human ego will certainly make every effort to place itself above all those "lesser important" life forms.

The human ego is the greatest impediment to unconditional love that can possibly exist. Humans have convinced themselves, that they are a superior life form. They are not, they are a life form. There is not an ultimate life form in the universe. For to say that a life form is ultimate would put a limitation on God, which would mean God is not God. Therefore, those humans who honestly see every life form as a part of God, different, but co-equal with every other life form, and rejoice in the differences, and treat every life form with respect, and with the understanding that life forms are co-equal and co-important, are more capable of unconditional love.

As we evolve in our spiritual nature and path we will also have a better understanding in approaching the reality and goal of unconditional love. It will be the ultimate power, energy, existence and joining with the Oneness of the Creative Spirit of the universe. There is in true reality, only love and with our evolvement, all other activities, emotions and realities will fade into the pure energy of love, "the ultimate high", and goal.

Universal Spiritual Law of Love and Healing

Love means far more than human understanding conceives it to mean. Universal Law is complicated, unconditional, without demands, without anything except the motion, the creative energy of love. Universal Law of Love commands that every life form love itself without condition, by virtue of being a part of God, a creation of God, a child of God. You may word it however, you choose, but that is the ultimate truth. There is One God and God is Love. Love of course gives freedom of choice to oneself and to all other life forms. In an unconditional love of self and the true recognition that self is at One with God, a part of God, not apart from God. If a person is loving themselves correctly without human ego but with a natural and divine desire to be healthy, because it is a loving thing to do to self, then health naturally follows. This is God's law and can not be broken. Persons with healthy self-images, recognition of their own unique being as a part of God, manifesting in a physical aspect are always healthier than those with a poor self-image and a need to punish themselves because they feel unworthy. Love is a feeling of worthiness. It is natural not to wish to hurt someone that you love. Any hurting is not an act of love, therefore if a person has a healthy image of self, recognizing that self is worthy of love, self is a part of God, this will result in mental, emotional, and physical health and well-being. When one does not have a good self-image one will continue to experience physical difficulties for one reason or another. There are as many reasons why humans become ill as there are humans to become ill. Each human is carrying something within their consciousness that is interfering with purity of love. It is that simple. Pure love is healthy in every way. Altered love naturally leads to discomfort of the emotional and physical self. All disease results

11

from not loving self because self does not believe that it is worthy of love. Traditional religions have much to do with this also, for many of them teach their members that they are loved by God through grace, but that they do not deserve it. You were conceived in sin, born in sin, and are sinners who can only be saved by the grace of God. Thus we begin our human life being told that we don't deserve anything and thus a poor self-image is a natural by-product of being told that one is a sinful being. Humans are taught that sin should be punished. Ill health is most assuredly punishment. The sinner may not cease to sin, but at least at some level of consciousness they are aware that they are getting exactly what they deserve. They are being punished for their sins. When one comes to love themselves, as they should, and through this, to love all others, as they should, they realize that there is nothing to be punished for. They need not be ill, for they love themselves and see themselves as part of God. Upon occasion when they may do or say something that they know is not loving, they may experience some brief or even lasting physical condition. But usually, if a person has reached the point, that they understand that they are truly a part of God, if they begin to feel discomfort they can immediately find what they have thought or done that is not truly best for their health and through prayer and forgiveness of self and forgiveness of others, are able to have a rapid and complete healing. Thus part of love is knowing when you have been unloving to yourself. Unloving to one self includes doing things that are hurtful to other people with the desire to hurt them. This is bad for self, it is unloving for self, it is unhealthy for self. The whole thing then is to know thyself, love thyself and good health must become a part of your life experience.

Comments/Examples Law of Love

I would now like to briefly discuss two illustrations of love promoting healing. First recall the example I gave concerning the patient that created severe pelvic pain. The pain arose from her not loving herself but instead she degraded herself and felt she deserved to be punished, and she did in the form of physical pain. Only when, she realized there was nothing to be punished for, did the pain go away and her daily life and relationship became rewarding and happy. So by respecting and loving herself, healing occurred. As I said earlier, love is the ultimate healing energy and power.

A second example of how poor self-image and lack of self-love can cause significant symptoms such as pain, bleeding and etc. instead of physical abnormalities of the patient. This is best illustrated at the time of surgery. It is relatively common to operate on a patient with significant debilitating pain and at the time of surgery find absolutely no abnormal findings or anatomy to explain the cause of her symptoms. Pelvic organs uterus, ovaries, etc. are removed and the pathology report reads normal. Yet after the patient recovers, all of her debilitating symptoms are gone. If they believed the surgery would cure them it certainly can. This case is opposed to the patient with similar debilitating symptoms, but at the time of surgery, I would find endometriosis, scar tissue, cancer, cysts, etc. In other words, physical findings for the symptoms. As mentioned earlier, truly loving yourself, leaves you no room for poor health.

The last example I will give you involves the birth process. Unfortunately, a large percentage of pregnancies are not planned and many of those are not really wanted. Sad but true. The real joy in my OB practice were the parents who had a very loving and stable relationship and planned their pregnancy in a very loving way. The best example of these parents were the ones that wanted an underwater natural birth. Their love for their unborn and then newborn child was very evident throughout the pregnancy and birthing experience. The unborn truly knew they were deeply loved and their behavior at the birth fully reflected that emotion. (In my next book I will go into detail about communicating with the unborn and newborn child and all they revealed to me.) These newborns did not cry at birth and they were very observant and responsive as a newborn. So love truly gave them a non-traumatic, calm and joyful entry into this physical world. So no birth trauma needed to be healed. The healing came with the love given by the parents. This is opposed to the unplanned and unwanted newborn that loudly fussed and cried at birth and after.

2

UNIVERSAL SPIRITUAL LAW OF ATTRACTION

The law of Attraction, which is a very powerful law, states that what any aspect of the consciousness of God sends forth in thought form will return to itself. What you give returns to you or what goes around, comes around. The law is also a basic part of the physical creativity of the universe. Without the Law of Attraction, nothing in the universe could continue to function.

Let us discuss what would happen if the Law of Attraction were not always in absolute control and effect at the physical level. Imagine, if you will, our planet not continuing to orbit the sun in its current pattern. This would throw the entire solar system out of balance. The attraction of each planet to every other planet, to every asteroid, to every moon is a constant thing. Although it is a changing thing. Thus if the earth should suddenly go erratic, there would be destructive forces let loose within our solar system which would have the capacity to destroy the system completely. Thus, the Law of Attraction maintains each physical object in its perfect co-relationship to every other physical object.

The Law of Attraction is however mutable in the sense that the orbits in a given star system do constantly change in relationship to one another. Our solar system is undergoing a physical change at this time. Earth is changing the axial tilt of its own basis. This happens from time to time in any star system. Planets change the way they rotate upon their own axis. At the same time earth is also slowly changing its orbit around the sun. We now have a very elliptical orbit. When the present change is completed our planet will have less ellipse in its orbit and will become more circular than it was. Our galaxy is changing its orbiting around and about other galaxies. Change is a constant thing, but it is always governed by the Law of Attraction. The Law of Attraction makes certain that while the changes are occurring they do not become destructive, and thus demolish the galaxy. Thus, while the Law of Change is also in effect, the Law of Attraction maintains that the change not become a destructive menace to the physical expressions of creativity.

The Law of Attraction, in every sense, is responsible for reproductive activity in whatever form it may take within all species. Humans are attracted to one another, and the desire to mate and produce more human beings is of course within universal law. The Law of Love and the Law of Attraction maintain a balance of physical life forms. All species undergo this in various ways. This is true throughout the universe, for creation is constantly happening. Various life forms are attracted, reproduce and maintain a balance. This is also part of the interaction between physical life forms and spiritual life form.

Let us take humans on planet earth for example. Humans follow the divine Universal Law of Attraction- meet and reproduce. From this comes the creation of a new human life. Simultaneously other humans following the Law of Attraction die and return to the spirit world. Thus, balance is maintained between that which is physical and that which is spiritual.

Persons upon our planet earth today, from time to time, express concern that the earth is being over populated with human beings. This is in fact not the case. When humans learn to live in harmony with all life forms upon their particular planet they will find that Mother Earth is capable of sustaining much more life than most scientists believe to be possible.

People are concerned that the diminished amount of petroleum upon our planet will have an adverse effect upon human life. The diminishing resources will change the way humans live, but not adversely. Concurrent with the diminishing of petroleum and other so-called fossil fuels, the Law of Attraction is drawing human beings into Aquarian Age consciousness in which, when it is fully expressed and realized, the instantaneous creation of something physical will be a natural thing to humans. They will not need to rely upon mechanical technology. This is an interesting thing to watch when any group of life forms can experience this and work with it. Then comes the recognition that the universe is a huge enough place to support truly a limitless number of any kind of life form. The Law of Attraction operates physically and metaphysically and inevitably draws the physical life form into metaphysical thinking. This is a natural evolution of all life forms. You will find that this great Law of Attraction makes certain that everything is kept in perfect balance.

The humans have eliminated from our planet many other life forms. Many people are very distressed by this, and they should be from the point of view that this has been done to make humans more comfortable upon the planet. From the broader point of view, all physical life forms have a limited existence. Life itself is limitless, but form is not. Therefore, even before humans resided upon our planet, life forms were becoming extinct, and will continue to do so. While humans and non-human life forms inhabit the planet together, humans must learn to coexist in love and harmony with the other life forms. If they cannot make this evolutionary leap, guided by the Law of Attraction then human life itself will cease to exist sooner than it needs to upon planet earth.

As stated, the Law of Attraction figures prominently in family and reproductive matters. For instance, one and their mate had an attraction to one another that drew them together. Something about one was similar to something about the other and equally true in the opposite direction. Therefore, they come together, join and remain until that which had been an attraction ceases to exist. Children are likewise drawn to the parents that they choose in this life under the Law of Attraction. Something in the parental beings attracts the spirit to those two particular people for purposes that will be of value to all of them. There may be a greater attraction to one than to the other, but the attraction must be to both. This is true also of adoptive children. They choose their birth parents for lessons that they may learn through the brief time they will spend with their natural parents, but the attraction to the adoptive parent will eventually place them with the chosen adoptive parents. Although this is not always a permanent thing, and it is sad when laws of man interfere with the laws of God, and remove a child from its adoptive parents. In fact the adopting parents are the ones with whom the child should spend its formative years.

Therefore, as you consider the Law of Attraction think again about your own family. Your attraction to your mate, and their attraction to you. Your attraction to the animal members of your family and their attraction to you. This is a natural thing, that life forms should be attracted to their own kind for reproductive purposes, and to other life forms for learning purposes, as to understanding the thought processes and needs of other life forms.

Another way to state the Law of Attraction is you reap what you sow. Many people don't realize this in this day and time of blaming everyone else for adversity in one's life, instead of taking responsibility for the happenings in their life (the Law of Responsibility will be covered later-again demonstrating the laws interactions) so it's obvious that wisdom would dictate that we should all send out very positive loving thoughts and deeds, since in one way or another we will not escape their return. We should all be reminded of the boomerang. So set yourself up for very positive and beneficial "returns". When one gives love, you receive love in return. Make no mistakes you will not escape the return of what you have sent forth at sometime in the future.

Every thought you have affects your being mentally, emotionally, spiritually, physically, financially, and in every way. Every thought you have affects the entire universe in either a positive or negative way. Every thought you have produces a result that is either physical or non-physical. There are no random thoughts. If the thought is loving, the result will be positive. If the thought is unloving, the result will be less positive, and perhaps extremely negative. Thoughts going forth begin the process of creation. Those whose thoughts are often a negative and unloving matter, draw to themselves an increasing degree of misery, joylessness, and indeed physical suffering. You cannot think negative thoughts without the result of those thoughts affecting your life, body and health. Neither can you think positive and loving thoughts without the results of those thoughts affecting your life. Your very being is affected by every thought you have.

It is important, to know that when you become impatient you are creating a negative vibratory energy which creates a barrier between you and the thing you desire. It can be a very physical as well as a metaphysical barrier. Impatient people often make mistakes. For instance, if one is using a computer, and they are eager and impatient to complete a project they will make more mistakes then if they enter into it with the gentle notion that the project will be completed in the best and most efficient manner from a calm point of view. As they use up more and more pieces of paper, or erase their mistakes they have a physical barrier between themselves and the project they wish to complete.

So, it is not only that a metaphysical barrier is created by negative thinking but physical ones are also. When a person is angry, they are not able to think clearly and their mind is not working in the most positive and practical way. They may do things in destructive ways. This only leads to more anger, impatience and frustrations. Physical things may be destroyed in anger or harmed in anger, thus the angry thought produces a very negative reaction, response, result, up to and including physical violence to the point of physical death as a result of anger. Each thought is a fertile, growing, living changing thing. Thoughts are not static. Since they are producing results, they must be considered changing things, for it is quite evident that the results of one's thoughts produces additional thoughts. Now, on the positive side, when thoughts are tranquil, peaceful, loving, joyous and free of negative things, the results then are ever changing and the individual becomes more and more spiritualized, proceeding in a calm and perfect fashion. The Law of Attraction is so very powerful that every thought has the potential to physically destroy the very planet we live upon, or to make it a flourishing place to live. Those who understand that what is sent forth must come back in some equal form, learn to monitor their thoughts. What is also discovered is that although the form is equal, in that like attracts like, the result is often greater than the original thought would seem to be.

What then can a human being do about being in harmony with the Law of Attraction? Because it is so powerful, because it begins with thoughts, which create results, each person must learn to monitor, not only their words, but every thought pattern, so that when they think a negative thought and know they are under God's Law of Attraction and something will come back to them as a result of that thought, they must transmute the thought into a thought of love. Therefore, when you are aware you have had such a thought, you think instead, "I AM SORRY, I FORGIVE MYSELF FOR THAT THOUGHT AND I SEND LOVE INSTEAD."

It is that simple to change the thought. You have now sent out a loving thought, and as you know love can move all things into itself, thus you have made certain that you will not be injured by your thoughts, nor will other people be injured by your thoughts. The thoughts that we think, affect us and affect whoever might be touched by them. The unkind thoughts that you might have for a person might not touch them for they may have a shield of love around them that protects them from your thoughts. But another unprotected individual may receive that thought, and be adversely affected by it, because they have not yet learned to keep themselves surrounded in a shield of love. Thus, it becomes necessary with each thought, that you program a portion of self to notice when you are thinking negative thoughts and to transmute them into love in a conscious way. This must be done consciously, you must consciously know that you have been out of balance with the Law of Attraction, and must come into balance with it. It must be done as quickly as possible for the benefit of yourself and everyone else.

There is a short cut that will keep you in closer harmony with the Law of Attraction. AT THE END OF EACH DAY PRAY BEFORE YOUR SLEEP AND FORGIVE YOURSELF FOR ANY NEGATIVE THOUGHT YOU HAD DURING THE DAY. FORGIVE ANY WHO HAVE HAD ANY NEGATIVE THOUGHTS TOWARDS YOU, WHETHER YOU KNEW IT OR NOT, AND THEN SIMPLY

THINK OR SPEAK ALOUD THE WORD LOVE THREE TIMES. YOU WILL SAY IT NINE TIMES IN THREE SETS OF THREE. You have then sent enough loving energy out into the etheric waves to transmute whatever thought you have had into love, and to keep any damaging effect they may have already had to be reversed. This does not release you from monitoring your thoughts, but we also have unconscious thoughts that are not completely loving, and so therefore we must all, at regular intervals transmute our thought for the benefit of the entire earth.

Lets take a common everyday example of a couple's relationship. In this day and time, maintaining a relationship is a real challenge. Most couples have much in common. The strongest thing, of course is the inevitable Law of Attraction that caused them to find each other desirable in the first place, and led them into the decision to share their life as mates and eventually as spouses. Each of you at your most basic soul level saw qualities in the other that were admirable, and which each felt they did not fully possess. Each of them desired change, or they would not have come together. The Law of Change also brought them to one another. In this natural progression of evolution, the two brought to their relationship things that each desired to share with the other. It is needful that their soul understood this, but the human part sometimes resists. Recognize that a relationship always includes the element of need, any relationship.

Therefore, instead of working enthusiastically to fully understand one another, couples occasionally are critical to one another. In other words the very things the couple came together to accomplish do not always get accomplished as rapidly as they might because criticisms, stubbornness, etc. measure in.

There is but one way to correct this, that is do what could be described, although it is not a universal law, law of attention.

When two persons have differing viewpoints, each of them knows something that the other one does not yet know. Differing viewpoints provides an exciting opportunity to learn something previously not known. Unfortunately, most humans do not use every opportunity they have to learn something previously unknown. They are more apt to attempt to convince the other that their opinion or viewpoint is correct. This leads to arguing rather than learning. The way to learn is first of all to listen, and then attempt, through what you have learned by listening, to understand more fully the viewpoint of the other. You have now learned something new that may very well be of value to you, but you cannot know this unless you have paid scrupulous attention to what the other one has to say, and have made no attempt to change the opinion of the other one.

When any two people learn to do this together, much learning is accomplished. It is not necessary that either one change what they believe or change their opinion, it is only necessary that each one learn the other's opinion, understand it and respect it. When people learn to do this you can well imagine the excellent results. let us take the area of religion. Most wars that are fought are on a religious basis because humans do not understand another's philosophical religious beliefs. They vehemently disagree with them and they do not truly understand other's beliefs because they do not set down, listen, pay attention and try to understand. Rather, they attempt to convert and if they are not successful at this, they often attempt to kill. Much could be accomplished, just by understanding the religion of other people. Religion is a basic part of human nature. Humans have made it so, and having made it so, most humans are quite willing to declare that their religion is the only true religion. As long as this attitude is maintained, and there is no listening with attention to the thoughts of others, people will continue to bicker and war. Thus, you and your spouse may continue to bicker with one another until you have both accomplished perfect attention to what the other is saying.

This is not an easy thing to do, but it is possible. Think, when you attended a class or university, you listened to what your professors and instructors were saying. You desired to learn, you paid attention, you absorbed the words of those who had something to offer you, that you did not already know. Why did you do this. You wanted that information, that knowledge, and because you were paying to attain it. If spouses would give each other that same undivided attention from a total desire to obtain information they did not previously have, there would be no spousal arguing. Much discussion, yes, but arguing and attempting to make the other agree with you would not exist.

Briefly, one might ask, what about relationships that are rather violent or negative? There are obviously personal relationships that appear to be a rather negative relationship, however are based on need and due to ignorance in thinking, people feel that they need certain things, even punishments. An example would be the couples of spousal abuse, alcoholics, etc. These relationships have come together for a reason, so the Law of Attraction obviously is still in effect here, unfortunately the Law of Attraction is in concert with the subconscious ignorant thinking. Unfortunately, some people, think they need to come together so that they can be punished by one another. The real facts and reasons are usually buried deeply in the sub-consciousness and does not readily reveal itself.

This will continue to be correct as long as any person believes that they deserve to be punished and it's obvious that the world/people are over burdened with guilt, needing punishments (they believe). All of these things are governed by the Law of Attraction. Like all laws, Universal Laws, it is neither good nor bad, it simply is. How people react to, and act within that law is entirely their choice. If their choice, for whatever reasons is to act within the Law of Attraction by being attracted to daily violations through physical punishment of their physical body, so that they might learn, this is what they believe is their lesson, and they are obeying the Law of Attraction in what you would perceive in a negative way. To them it is a positive way because this is what they perceive as right for their particular need. It is very difficult, on the highest level to decide what is right and what is wrong.

All things are right in the cosmic sense, for everything is an opportunity to learn, a challenge to be met, a way to grow, a way to change. All of these are necessary until the thinking and guilt changes. So as previously stated, Universal Spiritual Laws are impersonal and lack emotion and judgement. All of that has been created by human thinking.

One aspect of the Law of Attraction might be thought of as starting out on the subatomic or molecular level of the universe. The Law of Attraction brings together the substance of the universe and forms it. Formless substance is essence of the matter or material substance in which all forms, or thoughts are created. Every creature that reaches form, whether the form is spiritual or physical is created from what might be described as the free atoms of the universe. The formless substance, through the creative thought pattern, is molded into form.

Let us begin with something simple, a human infant. The process of creating a child begins when the substance of the female egg, and the male sperm unite, life begins at that time. But what brings together all of the necessary cells, atoms, and molecules that eventually result in a fully formed viable human infant? Science has many explanations for this, but even they admit they do not truly understand. It happens from thought. The person who wishes to incarnate into a new physical body puts the substance together to form the new body. As the parents of the newly forming being become aware that a child is forming, their thought patterns add energy to the process, thus the continuation of the growth. The power of thought is the only thing that can attract formless substance into any form that is desired and Mother Nature takes it from there.

The Law of Attraction gives the right for thoughts to attract together the necessary elements to create something that is formed from formless substance. Constantly this formless substance is being attracted by thought to create form, and when that form is no longer viable, and it happens with all physical things, the decay sets in, and that which has been formed again becomes formless substance, to be reused in the formation of something else. The atoms that make up your current physical body have been recycled many times. Formless substance is an eternal thing and always available to become formed substance by the Law of Attraction, which brings the substance together to create.

So as one can see, the Law of Attraction has many aspects and is intertwined with the other laws. These laws are not manmade laws, which are a lot of disjointed does and don't to try to direct social behavior.

Humans have not yet reached the evolutionary state where they are even able to co-exist with other humans even minutely different from themselves. As a species we have not made this evolutionary leap in the Law of Attraction. This is the first things that must be done. All humans must follow the Law of Attraction, and respect and honor all other humans, before humans can be permitted to interact with other life forms.

There are those who teach or feel that opposites attract. This is not the case even though it may seem that way, particularly in some relationships. So, even though opponents seem to be involved, it is actually their needs that are attracting each other. For example, if you are hungry, are you not attracted to your evening meal? You are attracted to what you need. A male who is an extremely emotional and outgoing individual may be attracted to a shy and retiring female, or vice versa. It is because each individual needs to be with someone unlike themselves so that hopefully the emotional outgoing individual may learn to be quieter, more introspective and the shy, and retiring person may learn to be outgoing and allow their emotions to be expressed in healthy and positive ways. Remember, every person with whom you come in contact is a teacher to you and you are a teacher to them. Thus, two very different beings can be attracted to each other so that each might have the opportunity to learn. Sadly, it is not that the Law of Attraction is not in effect, it is that humans frequently deny these two humans the very opportunity to learn. Each overtly attempts to change the other rather than learn. This is not the way it should work.

Each should respect, admire and honor the quality of the other. It is an opportunity to learn what motivates a person to be shy and retiring, or emotional and outgoing. When two people see one another as teachers, lovers, companions, then each has the opportunity to enlarge their understanding, expand their horizons, which is what drew them together in the first place.

The thought that opposites attract is obviously a corollary to the Law of Attraction and very important one. For instance in many relationships, the people involved seem to be quite different or opposite, but they were attracted to one another because each had something to offer that the other needed. They both benefit from interacting with each other. Therefore, they both enlarged their perception, grew in consciousness, enjoyed the interaction and from their relationship both are wiser and more knowledgeable. An example of how Universal Laws interact is the Law of Attraction (what you send out, you get back) interacts with the Law of Need (needs create attraction).

Universal Spiritual Law of Attraction and Healing

Again, it is a well-known fact that whatever an individual does, has consequences. Consequences will be matching of what the person does, says, or thinks. You attract to yourself that which you send out from yourself. If the thought is; I am sick, then sickness is going to be what is attracted to the you. If the thought is "I deserve to be sick because I am a bad person and sinful person," the sickness may well become a chronic and to medical science an incurable illness. If one is a person who thinks more often in negative than positive ways, finding fault with self constantly or finding fault with everyone else, the energy that they are creating is an energy that draws to them illness. Negativity and illness go hand in hand. It could not be otherwise. Positive loving thinking draws positive energy, which creates healing energies within the body, strengthens the immune system and creates an attitude of good health and joy. The happier a person is, the more they have the potential to become healthy. Happiness breeds happiness and thus creates good health. Unhappiness, negativity, self-denunciation, dissatisfaction with everything and constantly finding fault with the way the world is, the way the next door neighbor is, the way the spouse is, the way the children are, naturally is a fertile breeding ground for any kind of illness.

There are only two forces of emotions: love and fear. Out of love comes positive thought of affirmation. Out of fear come all things that draw illness: guilt, hatred, fury and jealousy. When you have learned to think positive thoughts, speak positive word, then the Law of Attraction automatically draws to you more and more that is positive. Mental, emotional, physical and spiritual health is kept in balance. There are people who do nothing but complain. Soon they are physically ill. They then have one thing more to complain about, their constant physical discomfort. They become obsessed with their physical self and their illnesses. They dwell upon them, they complain about them, they talk about them, they allow themselves to become crippled by illness, by making a God out of illness. God is not illness, God is love. Humans can make God out of anything they choose. They attract to themselves viruses, germs, etc. Most things are not destructive to humans, but the value or power that you give them is destructive. It is likely the healthiest person on the planet has as much exposure to germs, viruses, etc. as the sickest person on the planet. They attract love because they are giving love. This is why they are so healthy, thus the viruses do not harm them, for the viruses themselves are transmuted into positive energy by the Law of Love and therefore cannot harm you. Nothing has the innate ability to harm. A child is not born with the ability to harm, they learn to do these things. Therefore, the Law of Attraction, saying so plainly, what you send out comes back to you, shows that if you believe germs and viruses, fungi, dust and mold and other life forms to be inductors of illness, they most assuredly will be. If you believe that all is God and no part of God could, by God's law, be harmful to another part of God, then no matter what you attract, where you are or with whom you interact, the illness will not trouble you, for you have not given them the power to trouble you. You attract negative energy into your body, because of your belief and because you gave power to that belief. Now you are in a position, where by only loving yourself and refusing to believe that any part of God can be harmful to you, can you be totally and permanently healed. The combination of medical science and metaphysical science is the way the cure will come for you. Humans attract to themselves many things. If you are a hateful person, you will be hated; if you are a loving person, you will be loved;

if you are a person filled with vengeance and the need to get even, you will find that no matter what you do, situations pop-up where vengeance is required because for you will be acting in ways that will allow it. If you believe you do not deserve good things, then you will only attract things that are not pleasurable. If you believe that you are the perfect child of God whose birthright is abundance it all things, physical and nonphysical, then you will find abundance coming to you, through the power of the Law of Attraction. That which is set forth must come back and by the Law of Multiplication, very often what one sends out comes back multiplied considerably, be it positive or negative. So remember your health and well-being originates in your thinking and beliefs. So be good to yourself and let love guide your life (thoughts, words and deeds) and love and good health is which you will bring to yourself.

Recalling the example of my patient with the severe pelvic pain, it shows how the Law of Attraction, as well as other Universal Laws, illustrates how her poor self-image and degrading herself created the attraction of what seemed the appropriate punishment (pelvic pain). She also demonstrated the positive use of the Law of Attraction after I was able to re-educate her and change her thinking. Her positive self-image allowed her to attract health and well-being.

I'm sure that you know friends or acquaintances that are always complaining about their aches, pains and illnesses. That's all they talk about and yes it does get old hearing about it. Stop to think, are they a happy and joyous person? Of course not. They are unhappy, complaining and joyless people. Their negative attitudes come first followed by all of the negative events and illnesses. The Law of Attraction, as all of the laws brings you anything you choose to draw to you, consciously or subconsciously.

It is truly sad and unfortunate that many religions teach and indoctrinate their members that mankind is evil and sinful, and deserves to be punished or condemned for their sins and even for eternity! I have been in churches that have this belief in their creeds they have the members recite during the church services. Do you really believe that an unconditionally loving God would teach its children this type of thinking that creates negative results throughout their lifetime? Of course not!

UNIVERSAL SPIRITUAL LAW OF CAUSE AND EFFECT

The Law of Cause and Effect states that for everything that happens there is a cause. Cause and effect are interactive with one another. That which is done produces an effect. The effect of something may not immediately be seen, but may, in time be traced to the cause. Very often the effect becomes pronounced before the cause is established. All things are a result of cause and effect.

The law is very closely aligned to the Law of Attraction but is a resulting effect. Let us begin with a simple and human example and then proceed to the broader. When two fertile and willing human beings come together in love, the effect of that love may very well be a new human being. The cause is attraction and love in most cases, the effect of that love may very well be a new human being. Cause and effect are actually one in the same. People see two things in action, this is the cause and this is the effect, but in fact, universally the cause and the effect are one in the same. At the moment that the act of love is being experienced a new life is beginning. There is no waiting period, the cause and the effect are simultaneous.

People tend to look on things as "I will do this and such a thing will happen." "I am the cause and such a thing is the effect". Because people believe in time they perceive it that way, but actually thoughts instantaneously create something. It just doesn't always instantaneously create something physical. For instance, one may desire to write a book. To the author there is a time between the research and writing and ability to make it a physical reality. In cosmic law, the book already exists. In other words the thoughts that the author has already been recorded cosmically. The book is being created as we speak. It exists as an entity unto itself in the spiritual world. It will eventually exist in the physical world. The cause and effect are simultaneous because every thought is a cause and effect of that thought spiritually, it's instantaneous.

Knowing this could promote people to monitor their thoughts more carefully, realizing that every thought they have, instantly produces an effect. The Law of Attraction enters in because the effect that is produced will be guided by the attractive factor of the thought that is produced. If you think a negative thought, a negative effect will happen too, either instantly or in human time. Like attracts like. Cause and effect is an interesting law and very important and they do not take as long to explain as the other laws because you can see in your own life so clearly that effect of your causal thinking. Your profession is the effect of decisions made previously. Whatever you are today, is the effect of a causal decision made previously. On the physical level people have a very strong understanding of cause and effect. When there is a war the cause and effect are easily understood and physically seen. The cause being that groups of people with different philosophies of life and have decided that they cannot coexist in the same physical space with one another. They, therefore will fight with one another and kill one another. It is a simple demonstration of cause and effect.

An example of the Law on the domestic front is the example of one striking their mate. You know if you do this you will cause physical, emotional and psychological harm, which will have far reaching results, certainly effects on the relationship. Therefore one would or should stop to think whether or not that would be the wise thing to do. Obviously the answer to that is no, to the effects which would result from the cause of slapping the mate. Therefore we may choose causes, with its resulting effect, so we can think this out before we act. If I do something, it will cause these effects, and do I want these or do I not want them.

Obviously the Law of Cause and Effect or in the language of physics, every action has an equal and opposite reaction, is not a complicated principle or law. The major aspect of the law is to help people realize their thoughts and actions are not isolated and unanswered occurrences. They all have consequences whether we choose to see them or not. But the wise person will make connection and more carefully consider the causes they create so the resulting effects will be of a beneficial nature. Obviously, at times it's difficult to stop and consider our thoughts and actions and remind yourself that they will come back to you. Particularly in the heat of emotions or at the time someone has wrongfully mistreated you or someone close to you. One should and can train their thought process to remind you of consequences, but this takes time and inner evolvement. Probably one of the main reasons many people don't totally accept and believe this law, is that in our society today, including "our system", it seems like all too often people seem to get away with everything, including murder, literally. Indeed, people often do not pay for their actions on a society or justice system basis, but you can be absolutely sure that the Law of Cause and Effect does not allow anyone to escape what they themselves have created by thought or deed. At sometime in their future all scales are balanced on a spiritual level.

To end this law on a positive note, be reminded to send out positive and loving "boomerangs." If you do slip, remember that negative thoughts and deeds can be transmuted into positive ones simply by the true use of love and ultimately by unconditional love.

Universal Spiritual Law of Cause and Effect and Healing

The Law of Cause and Effect is very similar to the Law of Attraction. They are twin sisters, although not identical twins. Every effect has a causal point. Good health is the effect of the cause of a good mental attitude. Where you live, what race, religion, nationality, ethnic group you are, has nothing to do with illness, for none of these things can cause illness. ONLY THOUGHTS, WORDS AND DEEDS CAN CAUSE ILLNESS. HATEFUL AND NEGATIVE THOUGHTS ARE THE CAUSE OF PHYSICAL, MENTAL, EMOTIONAL AND SPIRITUAL ILLNESS. THE EFFECT IS NOT DIFFICULT TO SEE. BY THE SAME TOKEN, POSITIVE AND OPTIMISTIC THOUGHT PATTERNS AND RECOGNITION OF ONE'S IDENTITY AS A PART OF GOD, CAUSE YOUR OWN INDIVIDUAL DIVINITY TO MANIFEST ITSELF IN GOOD HEALTH. Thus when the effect becomes apparent in either an emotional, mental or physical difficulty, the wise individual would seek to find the cause and attempt to work on removing the cause which has always been thought, word or deed. It is not always easy to find the cause since people are not always willing to dig as deeply as they should into their own soul memory which holds every thought you have ever had, every word you have spoken, every act you have committed or anything that has happened to you. It is sometimes necessary to do much soul searching to find the causal activity of a given emotional difficulty, mental difficulty, or physical difficulty. But with perseverance, the cause can usually be found and once the cause is found and positive energy applied, the effect will then become healthy rather than unhealthy.

When we refer to soul searching, that is exactly what we mean. Much more will be presented and discussed in my next book, but I will briefly touch on it here. Many times the cause of ill health cannot be found in the occurrences of this current life time. Also the fact that many people believe we only live one life time because that is what is taught by most western religions unfortunately, so we find physical causes for the affect. By spiritual design, past life details are not readily available to us, but they can be accessed by gifted individuals. Since our spiritual life is never ending and we live many physical lives, what happens in any past life time (mainly physical} can well play into health issues (or any other aspect of our current life) which will make it more difficult to place a cause with the effect. It could relate to hundreds of years ago. I have researched many examples of this during my many years of research. Logical but usually negative thinking, reveal the true cause. These examples and spiritual insights have given me great insights to how the Law of Cause and Effect really works. Just remember, if the effect is negative, the cause was negative. Until you transmute the negative thought, words or deeds into positive ones through love, the condition may not improve.

However over many generations we have come to find physical causes for our ill health and difficulties, which do play a part but are not the true original cause. The physical aspects (bacteria, viruses, cancer cells, etc.) are simply the mechanisms of illness and disease not the original cause. As an example of the misconception, many humans believe that the cause of flu is a virus which can be passed from one human to another, thus they see cause and effect as a physical thing and believe if they can remain isolated from any one with this particular physical disease they will not encounter it in their own life pattern. Belief in this may well help them to avoid the flu for a very long time, for they have put their faith in something. But it cannot work forever since they believe other human beings are dangerous to them and they must avoid the danger. That very belief creates fear which creates dys-ease and they may find themselves with the flu when they have done everything to avoid it. Another cause of physical disease is mass human consciousness, believing that certain things create certain effects and if they encounter one of these things it will be the cause of the illness. As long as vast numbers of people believe this, even a person who does not actively and consciously believe it, will be affected by it, for they are part of mass human consciousness. A good example of this happens each year when health authorities (CDC) announce the flu season will soon be upon us and since this has happened for many years, many people believe it and get the flu. This becomes a self fulfilling prophecy or "brain washing" in action that is perpetuated. If someone lived where they were never told about the flu or flu season, they likely would never catch the flu. It is very difficult to change mass consciousness.

So one of the ways to use the Law of Cause and Effect for healing, is to see all causal things radiating only from love. To see love as the one cause of the universe and to not allow, even subconsciously, a mass belief by humanity to lead you into experiencing discomfort or dys-ease. For many people it is a subconscious thing. They do not consciously think about a certain thing being a cause of a certain disease but subconsciously they may believe this to be true and thus could become ill. This is why the soul searching is so important and should be done fairly frequently to make certain that you are not harboring any causal misinformation that could lead to the effect of ill health. Again human choice enters in. Some people just "like" to be sick and they will find any cause for the desired affect and then boast of how unique their disease is. It is of course unique to them and it is of course their own creation. Their own effect, by the cause of their desire to be ill. Stop to think about what would cause people to choose "the sick role"? While being sick, people don't expect you to meet your usual responsibilities, you don't have to go to work, you may get attention and sympathy, people offer to do things for you and bring you things such as meals, etc. I would think that there are more positive ways to achieve these things.

Cause and effect also brings dys-ease into human relationships that cause the relationship to fail. There may be misinformation or fearful thoughts on the part of the one or both persons, in a relationship. That fear becomes an addiction and becomes the cause of the break-up of the relationship, the effect being the relationship becomes diseased and dies. The Law of Cause and Effect is in effect in every thought you have, every word you speak, every deed you do and must be recognized for the power it has in your physical well-being. Thus I would say, go to the primary Law of Love and make that the causal energy of your life and the effect will be ease, comfort, joy and health. This is the universal prescription. This law is relatively easy to understand, but one must be honest with themselves and take responsibility for all of their thoughts, words and deeds to make the law work in your best interest.

UNIVERSAL SPIRITUAL LAW OF FREEDOM OF CHOICE

This is one of the most important laws. Without freedom of choice nothing can be accomplished. Freedom of choice, simply put, means that in every area of every life form, choice is always available. It is an ongoing eternal thing and freedom of choice, or freedom to make a choice anyone wishes to make is eternal. It cannot be abridged, it cannot be changed, it cannot be manipulated, it cannot be infringed upon. It is an absolute eternal truth. With this greatest of all freedoms goes absolute responsibility for the choices that are made. This is obviously a very important part of the law that most people on this earth have chosen to forget. The choice they like, it is the responsibility they frequently do not like. Therefore in a very real sense we might say that freedom and choice are somewhat interchangeable. Freedom is choice, and choice is freedom. Without this immutable law nothing would happen, and in many of our world's great religions it is noted that God offered to humans freedom of choice. What is not made abundantly clear is the responsibility that freedom carries.

Generally, humans think freedom of choice is a choice to be either good or bad. Mankind has taken the mighty Law of Freedom of Choice and turned it into a conflicted law that says your choice is to be what I say is right or to be punished or that you have freedom of choice, but the choice is limited. That is so untrue. There are not words enough in every language on earth combined to state the untruth of that belief. Freedom of choice is in every thought, word and deed of every life form that inhabits the universe eternally. Choice is universal, choice is constant, choice is eternal, and there are always in any given situation multiple choices. Rare, indeed is it, that choice is less than multiple. That happens only when an individual has consistently made a series of choices. Let us be very specific now, to give an example: An individual has been involved in gaining spiritual enrichment. They have consistently made choices over a period of years that enriched their spiritual life. Eventually a time comes when they have great knowledge of spiritual things and great opportunities to use the knowledge. Knowledge can be used in any way, for positive purposes or very negative purposes. The individual has consistently made choices that have enriched them spiritually. As they continue to do this they reach what we call the point of no return, where every choice has so enriched them spiritually that they literally have lost the capacity to make a choice that would be negative in their spiritual evolvement. Thus through continuous positive choices, they can't make a negative choice, but they still have continuous positive choices.

Conversely, an individual might choose pathways of gaining spiritual information which they consistently are applying to their life in negative ways. Eventually they reach the point where they have gone so far on a negative pathway that they no longer have the capacity for change, at least in this particular lifetime. Therefore, they will return to the spiritual realm and be reeducated, helped to understand the choices that they made and the responsibility accrued by those choices, and choose other pathways of fulfillment.

None of this implies that either individual has reached the point where they have no more choices in their life. It only is to show that in a certain given situation points may be reached where choices in that situation become limited, for all choices have led to a firm decision, which will not be changed.

In freedom and in choice, all options are open. Freedom is full options. Freedom could not be less than full options, or it would not be freedom. Choice is equally limitless. If there are limits, it is not true choice. We are speaking then of limitless freedom, limitless choice, and that the two are really one. If you remove freedom from choice you have nothing. If you remove choice from freedom, you obviously have nothing. Therefore, we would say to think of them as freedom of choice, freedom in choice and freedom is choice and choice is freedom. They are so inseparable in the Universal Law of Freedom of Choice that we are incapable of thinking of one word without the other. The definition of freedom, then is simple, one may do, say, think, feel, believe, accept, reject, act upon, refuse to act upon anything, everything and all things in their entire life pattern, and in their sphere of life and in their interaction with all other life forms. All humans may do exactly as they wish to do at all times and under all circumstances. This is absolutely available, there is no limitation, there is only absolute and total freedom eternally.

Choice is the ability to decide between one action or another action or a number, a limitless number of different actions. It is absolutely unlimited. No choice is good or positive and no choice is bad or negative. The results of the choice determines positive or negative power or value of the choice. However, when you get into the consequences of the choices then you will be drawn back to the necessity to think carefully before making choices. Not to just say that, "I choose to do this because it is neither good or bad, but rather I choose to give careful thought to this, so while the choice is neither good nor bad, what happens may be positive or may be negative and

I am exercising my freedom of choice by choosing to think carefully and find a pathway which will lead to positive results".

Every choice has a response or reaction, whether it is a conscious choice, a subconscious choice or an unconscious choice, there is always a response or consequence. Therefore, the wise individual, aware that every choice he or she is making will have results in their life and quite probably in the lives of many other people, and in the universal sense in the life of every entity throughout the universe, will spend time following the Laws of Thought, Prayer and Meditation to find a choice that will be beneficial to self and to others. People will recognize that what benefits self, automatically benefits all persons involved and they will therefore accept that the consequences of their choice will also touch on many people. One would then wisely wish to use their freedom of choice which will not negatively impact on others, or on self. Freedom, choice and responsibility are three parts of a divine pyramid. When a person makes a choice to do something deliberately designed to harm another life form, the consequences show quickly, but the consequences to the individual who has made that choice, perhaps will take a bit longer to manifest themselves, but they will manifest. When a person deliberately and consciously makes a choice for negative activity they are harmed far more greatly than anyone else involved. Understanding this significant truth, it would seem that one would be wise and kind to themselves, by avoiding these kinds of choices.

Now, for the flip side of this coin, and something very hard for many to understand. When a person makes a decision after thought, prayer and meditation to do something that is righteous and good for them to do, but they know may hurt another, this can be a very difficult kind of choice. They must then rely on the metaphysical truth that if in every way the choice you are making is good and beneficial and positive for you, even if it seems to be something that will cause pain to another, you must make it anyhow, because it will eventually help the other. Let us use an example that is somewhat common: A couple is having domestic difficulties. The marriage is insecure because one partner is an alcoholic and refuses to seek help or even admit to the problem and is abusive verbally and or physically. The spouse who must make the decision has ceased to love the abusive spouse and wishes to enrich his or her life by terminating the marriage and beginning a different lifestyle designed to bring more harmony, comfort, joy, etc. into his or her life. The abusive, addictive alcoholic spouse has ruined his or her life, health, cannot hold a job, is unwell in every way. But refuses to do anything about it. The spouse wishing to change the life pattern, terminates the marriage, fully aware that this could possibly be the final thing that would cause the alcoholic spouse to perhaps terminate his or her own life, but realizing that the responsibility is still on the alcoholic spouse to either take charge of their life or terminate it as they choose. Years later the former spouses are in a position where they see each other once again. The alcoholic spouse has ceased to drink, has maintained a health pattern in his or her life, is gainfully employed, is happy and is even grateful for the termination of the marriage, for their recognition has come that as long as the abusive behavior was accepted by the spouse, the alcoholic spouse had no incentive to change. Thus, what seemed to be possibly the termination of a given life, instead really brought about a whole new life for both spouses. This has been happening with increasing consistency in our society, where as in the past, it was thought for many years the only choice was for spouses to remain together despite the brutality, alcoholism, drug addition and to hope that it would go away. However, when definitive action taken for a decision to choose happiness for one's self and a new lifestyle, it does benefit everyone.

These things are happening with increasing frequency and as a result many beings who would have continued in their addictive abusive behavior and shortened their life span considerably have chosen, when abandoned by their former, what you would call enablers, to take control of their life once more. Therefore, to sum it up again, when making a choice you have absolute freedom and absolute responsibility. You must examine the possible consequences of the choice you are making. That is your freedom to do. You must recognize that sometimes a choice you make may have any of several different consequences in our own life or in another's life. You must try and choose the one that has the most positive consequences for you as an individual and you must recognize that what truly benefits one individual benefits all who are concerned. This, then is exercising, living in accordance with, appreciating, valuing and certainly using in a practical fashion the Law of Freedom of Choice.

With freedom of choice we have an opportunity to learn lessons that will help us evolve to a higher level of spiritual development. We do this by learning from the choices we make and we most often learn more from our poorer choices than from our more positive choices. So our progression is never a straight upward path, but in enough lifetimes we hopefully learn from our choices, both positive and negative and make better and more loving choices that benefit us and the people and world around us.

Universal Spiritual Law of Freedom of Choice and Healing

Before starting on the healing aspects of the Law of Freedom of Choice, I would like to point out some very important aspects of this law. When God created the universe it was created in love, balance, harmony and perfection. When mankind was brought into existence, it was created in the same way. Life was perfect and there was NO illness or disharmony. As we can well see, mankind has developed an extensive ability to create these things in their life as a result of their thought, words and deeds. This was all done as a result of a loving and forgiving Creator giving us the Law of Freedom of Choice. We, over eons of time, choose to create disharmony, illness and disease and wove them deep into the fabric of our lives. How sad. Please stop and give serious open minded thought to this and hopefully, you will start realizing how you can start creating a life, as it was originally created, by changing your beliefs, thoughts and choices. This is obviously not an overnight process by any means and it will take many people to do the same. But remember, you are the one that has the responsibility and freedom of choice to directly change your life in a loving way.

This also should be considered, when people ask, "Why did God do this?" in a time of sadness or distress. This gets back to the Law of Responsibility (next chapter) and the fact that many or most people don't want to take responsibility for undesirable things in their life. Since God gave us freedom of choice, that means just that, you are the one that makes the choices that direct your life. Again Universal Laws cannot be broken, they simply are! Now to the Law of Freedom of Choice and Healing.

Every thought, word and deed is freely chosen. You may think you have impetuous thought, you do not, you have chosen impetuous thought. Everything is subject to freedom of choice. When choices are lovingly and wisely made, they are a significant important part of healing. The decision to be healthy and well must be made before health can be obtained and sustained. If there is any part of human thought process that is rejecting good health, then the human has chosen to reject it, whether it is consciously or sub-consciously. Freedom of choice is absolute and it is an absolute necessity on the part of humans to desire good health, to think positive thoughts, to use their freedom of choice to always think in loving ways towards ones' self. However, the majority of humans are kinder to others than they are to themselves and they do not love themselves as well as they should. They do not affirm or understand their own divinity as often as they should and do not perceive themselves to be as valuable as they truly are. Lack of self love, a choice that the humans make for various reasons, interferes with healing. For humans to begin the process of loving themselves and seeing themselves worthy and as an important part of the universe and to become healthier and remain healthier is a difficult process for humans to undergo. It doesn't seem as difficult for humans to use their freedom of choice to love others and thus help in the healing process of others who are using their freedom of choice to receive the healing. So in being able to see the vast importance of freedom of choice in healing self or helping to heal others, we must begin with a basic freedom of choice that the majority of humans are not choosing to take advantage of: the freedom of choice to love one's self, to perceive one's self as valuable, as a part of God and necessary to the universe. Without human ego involved, just an admission that "I am the perfect child of God" is freely choosing to accept the truth and the truth shall make you free.

Truth is the result of freedom of choice, truth is healing. Accepting this by your freedom of choice, the divine truth begins the healing process designed to create good health, maintain good health and expect good health. If at times the person doing this, allows their freedom of choice to let them become angry at self or at another, become depressed or unhappy, they have but to remember who they truly are and what they truly are, to return to that truth that is the result of freedom of choice. Whenever any illness touches a human, it is because they have used their freedom of choice to harm themselves. When healing is not occurring it is because they have used their freedom to choice to harm themselves. When healing is occurring it is because they have used their freedom of choice in its healing capacity. Perhaps the greatest gift the Almighty Creative Power of the Universe has given to humans and to all life forms is the gift of freedom of choice. It is a gift that humans must learn to use more wisely and more truthfully. For a human to make a choice to say, "I do not matter and I am insignificant" is making a free choice not to be all that they can be, not to be healthy in mind, emotion, soul, spirit and body.

Each individual has their own right of freedom of choice and they are permitted and encouraged to change their belief system, to freely admit to their own uniqueness and importance, to eliminate from their conscience that unhealthy belief that they were conceived and produced as a result of sinful behavior. All things that teach humans to not love themselves are the result of human choices freely made. They are not however true. Freedom of choice is a very powerful part of the healing energy when it is correctly used. The first step in using your free choice is love yourself and that seems to be the most difficult choice for the majority of humans to make. Please give deep thought and consideration to the above wisdom and insights and realize what unhealthy and destructive conditions we are taught to create within ourselves and our life. Make the choice to see and love yourself as a part of God. Begin an important healing process that will serve you well. Again LOVE is the ultimate healer.

5

UNIVERSAL SPIRITUAL LAW OF RESPONSIBILITY

The Law of Responsibility is that all aspects and life forms of the Universal Consciousness are responsible for everything they think, say and do and must expect the consequences of its every thought, word and deed. Responsibility is a law that helps every aspect of the Consciousness of God, the Universal Consciousness, to maintain its place in the structure of the universe. Responsibility is the law that governs thoughts, words and deeds in reference to what an individual wishes to resolve, create and handle in their life patterns. It is true of every life form. Responsibility is also a building block. It is a part of the basis of all creation. The Law of Responsibility makes each atom, each aspect individually responsible for their place in the overall consciousness.

If you will stop to think, do not all laws require a sense of responsibility, beginning with the very first law, the primary Law of Love, is it not taking responsibility? Responsibility is simple to state, not simple always to create. Why then do life forms all over the universe, including humanity, desire to evade responsibility and to get someone else to do it for them, or to blame another for whatever happens to them? This is simple to answer. It is easier that way! It is easier in the moment, but it only delays the evolution of the individual into its higher level of consciousness. The most stunning example of evasion of responsibility is sacrifice, be it sacrifice of another life form, or of one's own life form. Human sacrifice became very popular in the past and in some places still is. Because it was incorrectly believed that the sacrifice of another human being, or hundreds or thousands of other human beings would pacify the God of Gods and remove responsibility from one's self. Stated thus, it makes no sense, it is only more violence and more sin added to whatever the original sins were.

The entire Christian religion is based upon the premise that the sacrifice of one person, pardoned the sins of all humanity. Many accept this false belief, that all Christians are relieved of any responsibility for their own thoughts, words or deeds, because Jesus took care of it for all Christians. Undoubtedly, many Christian teachers and followers are going to take issue with what is being discussed here and in other areas of this book. And it is going to be a horrible shock and disappointment for people to be told that no one, not even Jesus, can take responsibility for their thoughts, acts, deeds and unfortunately their sins! This misrepresentation, be it intentional or unintentional, many centuries ago, is only one of probably many. Jesus died as a teacher and did not in any way pretend, or did it even occur to him that in dying he absolved anyone from any responsibilities, whatsoever, for any sins they had committed, or would commit. It is not my intent to take issue with established belief, but to simply present the truth as I have been taught. If you use simple logic, intelligence and think for yourself, you can reach whatever conclusion you choose. However there is only one truth that exists in the Oneness of God. However, the real truth often gets swayed, shaded or just plain changed quite often to serve someone's own agenda in a less than loving way. If you look within the goodness of yourself the real truth will be revealed.

All of us are here to experience things and grow as a result of the learning from our experience. We achieve spiritual growth in this manner, be it rapid or slow even though the rate doesn't matter. So, if you really objectively think about it, a very important saying that was given to me by my spiritual teacher makes perfect sense. That statement was, WHEN YOU TAKE RESPONSIBILITY FOR SOMEONE YOU MAY WELL BE ROBBING THEM OF AN IMPORTANT LEARNING EXPERIENCE. Stop and really think about the statement, and you should be able to easily see the great truth in it. Obviously, there are a few qualifications to this such as involving one prior to the age or ability to reason. So there is probably a fine line of distinction since even infants need to learn valuable lessons.

It is often difficult to find that very fine line, therefore, certain arbitrary rules exist that can help an individual to find the line. You are responsible for your child, until your child is old enough to be responsible for itself. We have set the legal age, in our country at 18 years old, when a child becomes responsible for itself until that time, you are responsible for your child to teach it as well as you are able to, to give to it the love, the care, etc. that it requires and then "turn it loose". You are responsible for persons of mature years who have reduced mental, emotional and physical abilities, strengths and well-being. It becomes the responsibility of the healthy adult to care for their aged parents, grandparents, and others who are unable to care for themselves due to advanced age. Beyond that, your responsibility to others is quite simple, you treat them as well as you are capable of threating them. You give to them opportunities to grow and evolve, as such opportunities become available. You advise them when they are acting in ways that are not to their soul's best progression, and other than that, you leave them alone to learn.

You are not responsible for the mistakes that others make, you are only responsible to advise and counsel them against the behavior which causes a mistake to occur. Your responsibility is to yourself. If a person is truly self responsible then their life can be expected to be lived in comparative comfort. When all are self-responsible, there will be no more crime, no more war, no more poverty, no more "unwanted pregnancies", no more mistreatment of other life forms and no more selfishness, greed or vanity. This is why the coming Aquarian Age is called the age of self-responsibility, for in it, the human race, for the first time in its history will become self-responsible, and the benefits of that shift in consciousness will be what is described as Utopia, enabling you to do anything you choose to do, go wherever you choose to go, to claim our heritage as galactic beings.

Let us look at several types of responsibility that we often talk about such as self, children, mate, others and country. The Law of Responsibility is, first of all the law of self-responsibility. If one is truly acting in a way that is completely responsible to themselves, and for themselves, the other aspect of responsibility follows in divine order. For example, as one recognizes their responsibility to themselves, to keep themselves healthy, well balanced, fit, in a loving, giving, and receiving and caring frame of mind for themselves they are also, at the same time observing their Law of Responsibility towards their children. Obviously, children need healthy, caring, well balanced and self-responsible adult human beings as a role model to help them understand the Law of Responsibility. You are also observing responsibility towards your spouse, for spouses deserve to have a happy, healthy, caring, and loving responsible mate. In good committed relationships each person cares for themselves and in so doing are providing their spouse with the best possible partner. Feelings of self-responsibility naturally include loving of other individuals for to give love is a healthy thing to do. To receive love is a healthy thing to do, and in caring for one's self and providing one's spouse with the best possible partner. Self-responsibility leads to responsibility in business relationships. Business relationships are too often based on selfishness rather than a genuine desire to have a prospering business that will benefit all individuals involved in the business. The truly self-responsible person recognizes that her or his responsibility is to give the business the attention, the education, the time, the devotion that is required to run a well established organization. In so doing they benefit from the organization, and all others benefit as well. If each partner is truly self-responsible they will do nothing to harm themselves mentally, emotionally, spiritually, physically, or financially. In doing so, they naturally contribute to the financial well-being of the business.

In terms of country, responsibility to one's country somewhat fosters emotions that are less than responsible. The idea of a country encourages the mistaken belief that being human entitles an individual to own part of Mother Earth in perpetuity. This, of course, is ridiculous. You can own a portion of earth, only as long as your physical body occupies it. You must pass such estate on to dependents, but there is also a limited time on this earth. The concept of country, encourages people to act in very destructive fashions that destroy self responsibility. Young women and men are encouraged through acts of violence against one another in "defense" of their nation. They are encouraged to give their life for their country or take others' lives in defense of it and they commit very selfish responsible acts, for these acts are detrimental to the progression of their soul. So you can see how man's creation of boundaries of land or groups serve to be very divisive to all of mankind, because segregation tends to foster emotions of superiority, domination, cultural and social differences. These often do not promote a cooperative effort and spirit, between two people who most likely simply want the same basic desires, wants and needs. Think about it, it does make perfect sense to the "common man"' but not to those in hunger for power and dominance.

Many groups have a belief system that often tends to teach that it is important to put responsibility of everyone else ahead of yourself in priority. It is often encouraged through the teachings that your rewards will be great if you do so. As one would expect, this quite often motivates people simply to do things for others in order to get whatever the promised reward might be, instead of truly doing things from the heart. Don't get me wrong it is important to help your fellow man but you have a priority or responsibility to yourself and those close to you first. Certainly one can meet responsibilities to self and at the same time serve others.

I'm reminded of several examples of responsibility. The first is the classic spoiled little rich child who gets everything they need and want and more without any effort. Usually things and services obtained this way are not appreciated or properly cared for and the child does not learn anything about taking responsibility for themselves and often makes for a selfish, thoughtlessness, insecure and unhappy person. We have all seen examples of this. Next is our current social legal system. Unfortunately societies' philosophy today is "you are responsible for me and anything that happens to me", thus all the often ridiculous lawsuits that are filed today. Very few people want to take responsibility for themselves, thus we have the conditions and problems that exist in society today. These will only start to improve when more people learn to start accepting responsibility for themselves, their actions and what happens to them.

Certainly our current welfare system is another travesty of taking responsibility. The system most often does not reward effort and pays more for doing nothing, or having added children that they can't support, instead of encouraging people to make an effort at bettering themselves and their family and at the same time improve or develop self-respect, confidence and self reliance. So taking responsibility for ones' self can be encouraged in many ways including welfare reform and not rewarding people financially or blaming others for things that happen to them. There is a very applicable saying concerning these points and that is, "Which is the most responsible act, giving a person a fish or the ability to fish?" Obviously that is a very easy question to answer. We and our government should not punish people for any act of self-responsibility.

Responsibility naturally leads to a responsible attitude towards one's family, friends, profession, place in the world, and desire to bring about improvements for all life forms. It covers, also the environment, the other life forms upon our planet with whom we share responsibility for the well-being of Mother Earth. So once one has taken responsibility for themselves, they can then help serve others. It's like you can't truly love others until you love yourself. So taking responsibility for yourself motivates self-betterment and change.

Ronald L. Cole, M.D.

Universal Spiritual Law of Responsibility and Healing

Perhaps the law of Responsibility is the most exciting of all natural law. It is also perhaps the one least used by a majority of humans. Without responsibility in some way there can be no actual healing of anything. A physician can go only so far in the healing process. They give direction, prescribe medication, perform surgery and procedures, tell people what is necessary or advisable to do, but they cannot make any of their patients do the things they suggest. It is their responsibility to follow the medical suggestions and orders that physicians give them. As we all know some do not do this, thus endangering themselves or others. So without personal responsibility healing is basically impossible on a long term basis. There are many ways that personal responsibility invites and co-exists with healing. It is true that some conditions can be corrected through medical techniques, but even that requires a sense of responsibility on the part of the patient to accept it. It is most distressing to we physicians, to give correct information to patients and find that the patients have not followed the instructions. Many reasons are given why patients did not follow the instructions, but the simple truth of the matter is they are not taking responsibility for their own well-being. Therefore I repeat, personal responsibility is a required part of physical, mental, emotional and spiritual well-being.

Now to be responsible means to desire to be healthy or to become healthy again. To take responsibility then is to do whatever can be done medically, spiritually and every other way to set goals for oneself in a responsible fashion and work toward the completion of these goals. To recognize that the human body is an ongoing work of art in progress, the person inhabiting the human body, the spirit, the essence, the soul is responsible for the body or the creation of this on going work of art, that every thought, word and deed creates a response in the physical body. Responsible persons wish to care for the body as a work of art and will have responsible feelings toward nurturing, feeding, resting and exercising the body. They will cooperate responsibly with physicians, psychologist, counselors, or whomever they may seek to help in the healing process. There has to be a responsible sense that this is my body and I am the chief creator and healer of my body. All physicians have patients who come in with a need, a discomfort, a pain, a health condition. The physician gives the attention and the treatment and the medication necessary and that condition becomes healed. But shortly, the patient comes in with a similar or different or the very same condition repeating itself. This shows that they have not taken responsibility. They have allowed the doctors treatment to temporarily heal the body but they have not gone that essential life-saving step, to take responsibility for the body. Thus no person who is not actively responsible for their body can enjoy good health and longevity. Now by actively, it does not necessarily mean only consciously but also subconsciously which may not be realized by their conscious understanding. The actual responsibility lies in the patient having a healthy mind, creating healthy and inspiring thoughts, a healthy life style, a proper diet, rest and exercise. This can be a consciously active or subconsciously active thought process.

Comments/Examples Law of Responsibility

You don't have to be a physician very long before you realize that almost all if your patients come to you so that YOU can heal or cure them and they can go their merry way with very little, if any effort on their part. Their effort is expected to only consist of keeping their appointment, getting a prescription filled, or possibly having a medical procedure or surgery and then all will be well. A major percentage of the time that is the way it works. So as discussed above, there is very little, if any responsibility taken on the part of the patient. This part of the healing "equation" has not been emphasized or understood by society. The main focus has been placed on the "healer" and not the patient. In true reality, the true healer and the patient are one in the same. Yes, we as physicians, can usually help in the healing process in many ways using medical techniques and principles. That is our responsibility, but the patient has not been taught the important and "bottom line" they play in their healing process. The fact that much of the true causes of what needs to be healed is on a subconscious level and unknown to the conscious level. There are, I feel and have learned, that there are very legitimate and accurate techniques to access this information. I will discuss this in detail in my next book as well as why people choose illness and disease and give a number of examples later on. Later on I will give you an example of prayers and affirmations that will help you program your thinking and actions to a more healthy life.

Over many centuries mankind has unfortunately been "saddled" with an evolving mass consciousness of what were claimed to be the truths of life that has based on what most benefited those of the ruling class for the purpose of control and power. These self-serving edicts have created the daily life beliefs and realities we now live by.

My patient previously discussed illustrated these principles well. When her family doctor inadvertently planted negative thoughts during her diagnosis, she created significant negative symptoms by guilt. When I re-educated her, she was able to let go of the negative self-image and take responsibility for healing herself. It sometimes seems to me that the word "responsibility" has been taken out of the English language. The various pointing fingers come out quick, all pointing away from their owner whenever a disease or "accident" happens.

When you take responsibility for all of our thoughts, words and deeds, you maintain control of your life. You may soon learn to stop for a moment before you think, speak or act and you will better control the outcome of these. I mentioned earlier the principle given to me by Quan Yin, "When you take responsibility for someone, you rob them of an important learning experience". No truer words were ever spoken. This certainly applies to the Law of Responsibility and healing since the one needing the healing must take the responsibility as well as have the true desire to be healed. Bottom line we all are our own healers. Of course we all also get help from the healing professionals. So most importantly you need to work at establishing an attitude of good health and the daily habits (diet, exercise, sleep, etc.) that will help you maintain your good health. It is indeed our responsibility to do so if you truly desire and feel you deserve good health.

UNIVERSAL SPIRITUAL LAW OF ABUNDANCE

6

The Law of Abundance simply states that there is absolute, total, unending, infinite and eternal abundance in the universe and every aspect of the consciousness of God may receive any degree of abundance in any way they choose to receive it. Whatever you desire, whatever you need, you create for yourself, by the creative power within you. You may have as much money as you choose to have. Money is something that you receive as necessary to your life patterns, and in your state of progression. You may be as healthy as you choose to be, you may be as rich in friendship and interpersonal relationships as you choose to be, you may grow spiritually, and have the spiritual abundance you desire according to your willingness to do so, and your creative ability. Abundance is creativity in action, nothing more and nothing less, than absolute creativity.

Humans essentially ignore the Law of Abundance and instead choose to compete against each other for worldly goods and abundance. The reason humans compete is because they believe that there are limited resources, there is limited abundance. They believe there is only so much of this and so much of that, and you must fight for your share of it. Thus, one country will invade another country because they desire what they perceive to be abundance of that country. We saw an example of this a number of years ago when in the Middle East, one country took possession of the other, because they believed that it would allow them to have the resources of that country at their disposal. This is limited thinking and competitive thinking. Thinking brought about by armed confrontation between the invading country and those who decided that they would help the invaded country.

Humans have done this for many thousands of years, and will continue to, until they realize that it is the mind that creates abundance. They do not have to take from someone else, in order to have for themselves. Out of your mind alone, you can create whatever you choose to have. Everyone has the power to create, unfortunately mankind has, over many centuries, developed a very limiting mind set. Therefore most people create limitations instead of abundance, and continue to deny the truly limitless creative power that we, as a part of the Universal Creative Mind, have always possessed. We need to quit creating limitations and instead enjoy the abundance of the universe available to one and all. We can do this by knowing with every fiber of our being that we are part of God, the primary creative source of the universe. You have infinite intelligence, and you know with every fiber of your being, that everything is God and is ever creating. When you truly know this, not just as a belief, not just as a saying, but as a knowing within yourself, and it is beyond any question, beyond any need for proof, that you can physically create whatever you wish or desire. The great Masters have done this and are still doing it. Most people have not yet reached that absolute consciousness of the Creative God Energy, and that is why they compete for what they believe to be valuable.

There is also another thing that holds humans back from this. It is religion. Many religions teach that God is apart from humans. But many thinkers are coming to the recognition that God is a part of all that is in creation. At the subconscious level we are still being held back from our fullest creativity by a subconscious clinging to the idea that God is, in some way separated from humans. We must open our minds and thinking to the fact that God is ALL of Creation or the Oneness of the Universe and that we are a part of that Oneness, not separate from it.

We have been given an excellent example of the creative ability of the human mind about two thousand years ago. Jesus the Christ often demonstrated this ability to create and remember He said "ALL THESE THINGS I DO, YOU CAN DO AND MORE!" Jesus did not concern himself with needs for out of the free atoms of the universe He could produce whatever was needful for Him or whatever He desired. He never went hungry, never went unclothed, never went without shelter because He knew whatever He wanted was already there and could be physically created at anytime.

Jesus was quoted as saying "Render unto Caesar that which you need and produce necessary monetary coins to do so". All people can do this, it is not a mystery how it is done, it is only that people have not yet, in their mass consciousness, recognized their absolute Godhood. When they do they will not produce a pile of gold since they can produce whatever the gold would have purchased. Yes, it is easy, but most of us have not yet reached that point in evolution where they know, at every level of consciousness their pure Godhood, and few indeed have accomplished that. There are but few Masters today who have achieved this level of spiritual evolvement, but in time the numbers will grow and all competitiveness will disappear. The competitiveness will take the form of the creative desire to expand yourself into the galaxy to interact with other beings to become part of the cosmos rather than confined to our planet. Creative abundance, the Law of Abundance is so very simple, and yet so few people have even a tiny understanding of it. Abundance is an infinite thing.

The universe, physical and spiritual has infinitely more abundance than can ever be used and it is constantly creating more abundance. When people and this planet cease to exist physically, all of their components will have returned to the free atoms of the universe to be again used to create other physical substances. NOTHING DIES, IT ONLY CHANGES FORM. The formless substances of the universe always are available, it is infinite.

Howard Hughes is a great example of this. He was one of the richest men that ever lived, and he had a very miserable, unhappy and questionable sanity life He died in squalor of mind, emotion, and spirit. All of the huge wealth he had collected through his competitive nature in his younger years was of absolutely no value to him later in his life and he lived and died in fear, isolation, squalor and wealth through competitiveness. However, if you have achieved your wealth through service to others, you cannot fear that you have taken from others or that they will attempt to take back from you.

On the other hand, those wealthy ones who have earned their wealth through creative thinking, through recognition of their own creative ability, have the capacity for greater happiness and joy in their lives. They have no conscious guilt because they earned the money through their own creative abilities. Creative thinking produces wealth that the creative thinker is free to enjoy in any way he or she chooses to enjoy it.

Let us look a little more in details to how one can begin to develop the attitude of abundance and the creative spirit that is truly in each and every one of us. The level of development or evolvement is a very individualized thing. Begin by eliminating the word "win" from your vocabulary. Winning implies that if one person wins, then at least one other must lose. You must eliminate competitive thinking.

Working on recognizing that abundance is infinite, you move

from winning to simply naturally acquiring all the abundance that you wish to have without any winning or losing. This is hard to understand due to many years of limiting programming that most of us are influenced by in our early formative years. When you absolutely know yourself to be a part of God through prayer and meditation, it would not even occur to you to think of winning a lottery. You would simply do the things you choose to do, knowing your abundance is assured, it is there for you, you are creating it with every thought.

The Law of Abundance is one of the most powerful aspects of the primary Law of Love, because the Law of Love requires that everything, everyone, every aspect of God be abundant. It is love in a very powerful and condensed form.

In summary the Law of Abundance states that God is the source of all abundance. You are a part of God therefore you create your own abundance. It is a natural thing to do, abundance is a part of the Law of Love. Abundance is an infinite thing.

There is no true abundance in competitive thinking. Competitive thinking says that you must compete for limited resources. Creative thinking says there is no limitation, resources are infinite. You must create your own abundance from the infinite resources of the universe, and specifically the infinite resources of our planet. There is no finite resource, there cannot be. That which you perceive is a finite resource, in whatever form it is experiencing life now, it is but a part of the infinite resources of the universe and will experience life in another form when it is no longer experiencing its current life. All that experiences physical life will cease to experience physical life in that form, but will not cease to exist. It will become a part of the free atoms of the universe to experience physical life as it chooses to, in other forms.

The formless substance, or free atoms of the universe, that you are working with is definitely willing to be formed into something through the power of your creative mind. There is also infinite resources as well as an infinite intelligence.

The Law of Abundance is one of the most powerful aspects of the primary Law of Love, because the Law of Love requires that everything, everyone, every aspect of God be abundant. It is love in a very powerful and condensed form.

Prayer for Abundance and Good Health

I will share a very useful tool I was given when asking how to help create abundance in my life. It is a very simple prayer. I added creating perfect health to the prayer since it is so important to our enjoyment of daily life. Say this prayer in the morning and in the evening.

First Pray the following:
- Thank you God for this perfect Day and what it has to offer in which I will learn things, experience things, know things and greet things.

Repeat three times:
- I am Light
- I am Love
- I am Devine
- I am the Perfect Child of God
- I am creating my own perfect Abundance and Health Now

Repeat two times:
- I give Thanks for the continuing creation of my own perfect abundance and health now and I share that perfect abundance and health with Mother Earth and all her children.

Pray Once:
- I ask to be forgiven for any negative thought, word or deed I have manifested that may have caused discomfort to any life form. I forgive myself for any negative thought, word or deed I have manifested that may have caused discomfort to any life form, I forgive any life form that has manifested any negative thought, word or deed towards me, and I give thanks for the gift of Forgiveness.

Universal Spiritual Law of
Abundance and Healing

This should be a favorite law, for most people since The Law of Abundance is the recognition that nothing is limited. Everything is boundlessly abundant. Recognizing this, a person can logically understand that if everything is limitlessly abundant, then good health must be limitlessly abundant for everyone, for every life form. When this recognition is a part of the consciousness of a person and they become aware of this wonderful Law of Abundance and recognize that it covers their very physical existence in terms of what health they have or what disease they have, a thinking person could choose to have abundant good health, abundant energy and abundant ability to do whatever they choose to do with their body. They would naturally choose the abundance of proper eating habits so they do not become larger than their body is best designed to be and choose the abundance of opportunity for physical activity to keep the body strong. They would also choose abundance of wonderful things to see, to read and to meditate upon. They would see abundance in every aspect of their life and their body would be healthy, vibrant and strong. Thus they would always be available for the next delightful thing. The Law of Abundance means that joy is in limitless abundance, that expectation of good health and happy things is in limitless abundance and out of their limitless abundance they would choose to be healthy. When persons do not understand that abundance is limitless, they may actually believe that because they have enjoyed excellent health until they are fifty or sixty years of age that it is natural to begin to deteriorate and so the body begins to deteriorate; eye sight, hearing, muscularity, organs and skin tonetic. deterioration. That same Law of Abundance says that deterioration is limitlessly abundant and so the process of deterioration goes on until the body can no longer function and the spirit leaves the body, but that is a false belief. The body responds to the mind and only to the mind. The mind gives information to the brain. The brain processes the information and uses it according to what it has received. If it has received the ongoing energy of believing that good heath is limitlessly abundant for an unlimited period of time, then the person can remain healthy as long as they choose to remain in a physical body. The body will not deteriorate and the organs will be fully functional. I'm sure most readers/people will find this hard to believe, but remember for generations we have been taught to believe in limitations. Therefore, it has become our way of life. Mankind has certainly "short changed" himself by his created belief system!

It is a belief among humans that at a certain age the female body ceases to function, for child bearing. Because they have created this belief, most women do reach a time when their body is no longer capable of child bearing and may develop bone deterioration, lung, heart, liver, and spleen problems. Eventually the poor women is but a caricature of her original healthy and vibrant self. She has chosen to give up limitless abundance of good health and accepts abundance of not so good health. Quite truly, in divine law, there is not a time frame connected with the ability to bear children. From the time a female becomes old enough to be capable of the act, she should be capable of it until she no longer chooses to remain in her physical body. The same is true of males under the Law of Abundance. The abundance of sperm that a male is capable of producing is quite limitless. There is more than the male can use in one life time, but there is also a belief that the abundance of sperm declines with aging. Since it is believed, it happens. An aged man becomes like aged women with certain parts of the body no longer functioning as they once did. There is no limit to their ability to procreate and produce an abundance of sperm. The human male's consciousness puts a cut off point on the Law of Abundance in procreation and vibrant health. It is also true for every organ in the body. Good health is in perfect abundance, limitless abundance, all the time. It is the responsibility of the individual to choose how much abundance they desire.

I know it is hard for most people to accept that there is abundance of good health since their mass consciousness of it being limited by age started to evolve many hundreds of generations ago. The ignorance (lack of knowledge) of Universal Spiritual Laws allowed the beliefs to grow until they were well entrenched in our culture and became our "reality". This is very unfortunate but true. As I have indicated, it will take a great deal of effort and thought changing to rid us of this self-created reality. However, if we don't do this "homework" and make an effort to change our belief, things will remain the same. We should choose abundance of all positive things, which brings us good health and joy.

Comments/Examples

Obviously since we have been taught/programmed for centuries that we are mortal man and apart from God we find ourselves rather limited. But with changing our beliefs and thinking we can evolve to a state of Abundance. It will take time, but it can be done and the evolvement will occur.

As mentioned above, your mind is in control of your physical condition and appearance. We have all seen examples of people looking and acting much younger or older than their chronological age. Their personality reflects the mindset that creates the older or younger look. You can be old at a young age or you can be young at an old age. A relative of my wife still mows his lawn, works a garden and sends us the most entertaining and fascinating emails from the internet and he is 96 years old. So an abundance of healthy habits and positive attitudes goes a long way in the healing process and is a rather simple process and principle.

Finally, I would like to share an illustration of abundance that many may remember. I have to give George Lucas, yes the Star Wars George Lucas, credit for this insightful example that I remembered from an early Star Wars movie. He obviously had many evolved and insightful ideas when writing his Star Wars movies. This example involved a bar/trading post somewhere in the galaxy. All kinds of galactic creatures would come into the establishment with some rather worthless object and want to trade it for something of real value. Each time this occurred the proprietor would never argue about the price. He simple went into the "back room" and came out with what the alien wanted and gave it to him. What actually happened behind closed doors was that the proprietor well understood and had mastered the Law of Abundance so he could simply create whatever the alien wanted out of the free atoms of the universe. So there was never any shortage of anything of whatever any alien wanted and the "exchange rate" simply had no meaning. I guess you could call the establishment "The Great Amazon in the Galaxy". Obviously George Lucas was way ahead of the vast majority of people on earth. We have a lot of catching up to do.

7

UNIVERSAL SPIRITUAL LAW OF HARMONY

The Law of Harmony states that all things in the universe are in absolute harmony with all other things. Nothing may be out of harmony even if to human sensitivity it seems to be. Harmony is that which makes all things in the universe act, react and move in perfect synchronization with all other things. Every single facet of manifested universe is in harmony with every other facet. All things move in their own perfect harmonious cycle. Without harmony there would be chaos, and disaster. The earth and moon, for instance would get in each other's way, to their mutual destruction.

Without harmony, the very animals of earth would not know with whom to mate, and attempted mating being incompatible would result in nothing living upon earth. Harmony is of course an aspect of love, and is that which keeps things moving in the direction that will create the maximum good, and prevent the disasters. There is no such thing as a natural disaster whether weather related or not. All inclemencies are the result of negative thinking. In other words, we create our own destructive weather and abnormal disasters. Therefore negative thinking is an attempt to interfere with the Law of Harmony. It is only temporarily effective.

Harmony expresses itself in the seasons, in night and day, in the astrological movements, in astrological ages, and etc. In the length of a physical life of various things, for harmony to remain, all things must change, nothing may remain static, that would be no fact of harmony. That would be chaos. Therefore, physical things grow, and mature, and release their spirit and begin the decay process. This is harmony in action. In all things there is harmony, it is not always possible to perceive it, but it is there.

Harmony, is of course vital to being able to create anything. Without the Law of Harmony nothing could be created, or nothing would be in correct conjunction with anything else without harmony. We would have total chaos, in the spiritual as well as the physical world. The Law of Harmony makes certain that all that exists in every universe is harmonious with everything else. Even when you cannot see it to be true, all of the universe exists in absolute harmony with another so that they might interact with one another without distraction. You can prove this to be true, certain sounds can be destructive to certain other things. A note produced at just the right vibration will shatter crystal, for instance. In medical practice it is common practice to break apart some of the kidneys and gallbladder stones by using what would have to be called disharmonies vibration which would cause them to shatter into smaller pieces and be more easily passed in the urine of the patient. Harmony, then makes certain that everything works with everything else without destroying everything else.

The Law of Harmony is a large part of musical enjoyment as well as for the enjoyment of being with another human being that seems to be in harmony with you. It is vital in creation and sustenance of everything that is, and it is among the least recognized of the universal divine laws. For instance, it is true that God is All, and that everything is a part of God. It is therefore true that there can be no discord between one part of God and another part of God. They are in harmony with one another. Many life forms in our universe do not realize this, and so mistakenly believe that something they have come in contact with is causing discomfort or disease. This is an incorrect belief that they are not in harmony, for example poison ivy. If a human comes in contact with that portion of God being expressed they will suffer discomfort, and indeed they do. But it is not because the manifestation of God, called poison ivy, and the manifestation of God called certain human beings are out of harmony with one another. It is a wrong, incorrect thought pattern of the human that causes the discomfort and the disharmony of his or her own physical being. When humans and all other life forms throughout the universe recognize that everything is created in harmony with everything else, they will stop trying to be out of harmony with other life forms, and thus will no longer suffer discomfort, disease and the irrational attempt to destroy anything, or anyone that they have falsely labeled as dangerous to them.

This brings up an interesting example. Let's say an infant or small child was lost in the woods, and it came in contact with poison ivy. Let's assume the child was young enough that it had not been exposed to the thought process of the accepted beliefs that contact with the ivy plant causes a significant rash. Would the small child get the "accepted consequential rash?" If the child had no previous negative "programming" in this or a previous lifetime concerning this ivy plant, it is unlikely that the child would suffer any discomfort from this. It is however likely that if the child were still in contact with the plant when it was found, the immediate response to the adult finding it would be, "Oh, my God, the child is in a bed of poison ivy, it will become ill." Then, the child would likely get the expected rash soon after its discovery.

Although every child born certainly comes into this world with a great degree of knowledge and wisdom prejudices, they do not often come in with preconceived prejudices against certain life forms. These prejudices are most often taught behavior from societies many misconceptions and prejudices acquired over many generations. I certainly don't recommend that you expose your child to poison ivy to test what I said, but it has far more credibility than you would think.

There are many physical examples of this harmony concept and truth. One very close to my heart and interest is the experience of labor and delivery, and the perception of discomfort that most people associate with it. Western societies' general concept is well documented by movies and television. It is always depicted as an out of control, painful, yelling and screaming experience. This is because most couples/mothers have been pre-programmed in many ways and don't choose to do the work and thinking necessary to create a very positive and controlled experience pre-programmed type of labor and delivery. Labor is work but does not have to be extremely painful.

I have seen an extremely wide range of different labor experiences, and most mimic the "expected" one. However, I have known some women who experienced little if any pain with labor. These women were either pre-programmed and therefore did not expect pain or they did their "homework" of preparation, education and positive attitudes as I taught in my practice, along with self-confidence, determination, support and love. Pre-programming and beliefs create most of our life experiences since they have been cultivated over many generations.

Obviously this principle of harmony works very closely with the Law of Creation and other universal laws that will be discussed later in this book and we will see how situations, life events, disease and all other things are created.

In summary, my many years of experience as an obstetrician/

gynecologist, the one biggest and most significant problems patients have is that they do not work in harmony with Mother Nature, instead they work against Her. As a result they experience significant labor pain and many diseases and ailments, not realizing that the true origin of these start with the thinking process and beliefs.

So, I cannot stress enough the importance of the Law of Harmony and being in harmony with Mother Nature and going with the Universal flow. The Universal flow is always there and you can go with it at any time and have a far better life as a result or you can go against the flow and find the trip much more difficult. It is always our choice as to the amount of harmony we allow in our life. Without harmony nothing else can be achieved. As we have said before and will repeat later, all of the universal laws are fully interactive and all under the umbrella of the Law of Love, so harmony will appear again during other laws.

Ronald L. Cole, M.D.

Universal Spiritual Law of Harmony and Healing

This is a law of such intrinsic beauty. When all is in harmony nothing negative can enter in. It is negative thinking which causes the body to become unharmonious, to have disharmony. The instant disharmony enters the physical body, it creates a pathway for disease. Harmony is having everything working in the same vibratory pattern, without any dissent. This is not an easy thing to accomplish. A harmonious body is a body in which part of that body is functioning in total harmony with every other part. Nothing is impeding the body's natural harmony. A body is by nature a harmonious thing. The heart in harmony with the lungs, in harmony with the arteries, the veins, the capillaries, the whole system in harmony, every organ doing what it is supposed to do, in conjunction with every other organ. Every part of the body functioning perfectly, for harmony is perfection. What causes the body to not be harmonious with itself? The usual suspects, thought, unharmonious thought such as guilt, fear or anger which are not harmonious things. When negativity enters into the thought process, the body reacts instantly with a substance which, when directed by fear, creates what is called the "fight or flight syndrome". But adrenalin in overproduction, creates a lack in harmony in the body. If a person is constantly fearful, they are constantly producing adrenalin. This creates a lack of harmony between the adrenal glands and the rest of the body and the glands can then become destructive things, rather than a useful thing. Fear, the ancestor of all negativity, crates disharmony in the physical body. Remember that disease is a reflection of internal dys-ease. Harmony is maintained by positive thought patterns, by beginning the day in an up-beat and joyous fashion and by sharing that joy. Harmony is an aspect of joy and joy is an aspect of harmony, the two work well together. Harmony, of course, is created by love, the Great Creator. Think of the times when you and an individual have had moments of intense harmony in a relationship that you share. What a wonderful feeling of peace and joy overcome you and whoever is sharing this perfect harmony with and what a shock it is and a disappointment when something occurs, be it a thought or a deed, that removes the perfect harmony from the relationship. Very often people become physically ill because of such an occurrence. Disharmony causes physical illness. If a person is working in a situation where there is not harmony between co-workers, the body will eventually become ill, for the body cannot handle constant lack of harmony. The body is designed for every part of it to work in total harmony with every other part. If mental or physical stress is being placed to a degree that the body can no longer handle it, then the body becomes diseased. We have observed people, for instance, who are obsessed with the idea of growing a much more muscular body, actually more muscular than their skeleton is designed to handle. They do things to the body that displaces the bodies harmony. They work out more often than they should, they may put substances into their body that they believe will make them stronger and more muscular. These substances, which taken in large doses are destructive to the body and will eventually cause the body to be very ill and will also affect the mind. For while the body is designed to be able to, though the immune system, throw off most of the things it encounters that are believed to be negative things, it is not designed to be abused through improper usage. This is showing a lack of respect for the body. A person that is in harmony with themselves and their universe, will respect their body and will not deliberately do things that the body is not designed to do. The same is true of persons who eat enormous amount of food thus adding to the weight of their body beyond what the skeleton is designed to handle in harmony. They have placed a note of disharmony into their body, and it reacts by becoming weakened. It can not support all that weight and the person often has back problems, hip problems, leg and feet problems, breathing problems, heart problems, because they have abused their body. They are not operating in harmony with the body's natural abilities. Therefore they may well find themselves in great discomfort through disharmony of the body. A lack of harmony in one's life, causes one to build a wall against the world. Those who are seriously overweight have built themselves a fortress against the things that have hurt them. Instead they could deal with these things and create a harmonious and loving energy that would help them reduce or eliminate the hurt. This is one of the many ways we can abuse our body and create disharmony. Thus the body's harmony is essential to the body's health and well being. Loving the body, caring for it, feeding it properly, exercising it, resting it, and other normal behaviors are within the Law of Harmony which says everything must fit together to make a perfect whole. Think of your body as a musical instrument perfectly in tune, harmonious and ready to join in harmony with other musical instruments. It rings true when you touch the string or blow, or play the keys because it is properly tuned. Nothing out of tune can be in harmony. Treat your body with respect and love it as you would a Stradivarius violin, a perfect example of harmony when properly tuned and cared for. Harmony within comes from harmony of thought. Keep your thoughts clear and pure and positive. Treat your body with the respect it deserves with thought, words, and deeds. Love your body crated to be an instrument of harmony and it shall maintain its natural creative energy and good health.

Comments/Examples Law of Harmony

Briefly, recall my patient examples who created disharmony, therefore severe pain, due to the negative thoughts (guilt and poor self-image) "planted" by her family physician. Think of the miraculous perfect harmony demonstrated by planets in a galaxy, the formation of plants, the human body and fine-tuned machines to mention a few examples. Without harmony they would not exist. Obviously harmony is a very intricate part of the healing process.

8

UNIVERSAL SPIRITUAL LAW OF VIBRATION

The Law of Vibration states that each and every aspect of creativity vibrates at its own perfect level. Vibration is action and everything is always in action and it is in action perfectly with every other aspect of the consciousness of God. The vibratory pattern may be very distinguishable or indistinguishable. The vibration is that which actively keeps creation going. Vibration, in the simplest possible terms, is the rate by which all things exist in harmony with all other things. Every life form has its own particular vibratory rate. I will use a simple example of how the Law of Vibration shows itself in physical ways. If you are to examine the contents of a washing machine when it is washing the clothes, you are able to see action. The suds, the individual garments and the machine moving. You are able to detect color and form. This is a very physical manifestation of vibration. When the machine enters into the cycle in which the clothes are no longer being washed, but are having their moisture removed from them, the vibratory rate increases dramatically, and you are no longer able to see anything. The picture becomes blurry. You are aware that there is motion, but you can literally see through the glass door on the front of the machine, and only detect motion. There is no color, there is no form, for the speed has increased to the point where it is not possible to see individual things, and it looks as if the clothes are no longer in the machine, and all you see is the whirling action.

This is a very simple explanation of vibration in the physical sense. Spiritual rate of vibration, or in simple terms, the speed at which spirit moves, is very rapid and is not detectable to the physical eyesight. It is detectable to the spiritual eyesight but you may not be aware that spirit is near you. Even as if you were to touch the washing machine in its spin cycle you would feel with your fingertips, the movements of the machine, but you would not be able to see the clothing.

So it is with things that vibrate at a speed that is not detectable to physical vision. In order for you to see a spirit, or any other life form that vibrates at a speed that your physical eyesight cannot perceive, that lifeform must slow its vibratory rate to be seen physically. That which is perceived physically is vibrating at a slower rate. This does not mean that which is seen physically is less good, less spiritual, less divine than that which is vibrating at a more rapid rate. It only means that it is different, spirit is not better, but merely different than physical humans.

Now, this Law of Vibration literally holds the physical world in harmony. Each physical life expression vibrates at its own perfect rate in order to maintain the integrity of its physical body. This is true of a grain of sand, it is true of an atom, a molecule and it is true of the physical universe. The physical universe, as an entity in itself, is vibrating at its perfect rate of speed to hold all of its components in a physical state of being, and in relationship to one another. Were our planet begin to speed more rapidly in its axial rotation, the consequences would be detrimental to the life forms upon the planet, or to the planet itself. The life forms would not be able to sustain the vibratory rate, and would cease to exist and the planet itself would whirl to such an extent that it would cease to exist as a physical entity. Therefore, the Law of Vibration is the Universal Law that holds the physical integrity of the physical world, and the spirituality of the spirit world in proper balance.

All beings, although maintaining their vibratory rate, are capable of increasing that rate to a point where they are still not going to be damaged by it. Under certain conditions when a human being, for instance, is undergoing a very high level of spiritual ecstasy, the physical body will vibrate, but only to the point that the being can experience without damage to the physical essence. As we evolve spiritually our level of vibration will increase.

Most people have not yet had a physical experience of pure spiritual ecstasy. If you continue upon the pathway of determination to grow spiritually, a time will come when in prayer, or meditation, or some other triggering aspect in your consciousness, you will feel extreme sensations of spiritual and physical ecstasy, which will cause the body itself to vibrate, in the same sense that if you touch the string of a string musical instrument. The strings vibrate, but it does not vibrate past the point where its integrity can be maintained. When you experience this, you will certainly enjoy the experience. When you leave the physical body to return again to your spirit form, one of the things you will become aware of is that through the work, the spiritual learning that you have accomplished in this life time, your spirit body, which has its own memory of what it feels like to be a spirit will feel different to you. You will recognize that it is vibrating at a different level of speed than when you last inhabited it in the spirit world, or created it. Thus, the Law of Vibration is critical to the maintenance of every life form, be it physical or spiritual, and it works with the Law of Harmony. For the Law of Harmony and the Law of Vibration together keep all beings and all groups of beings working in their individual correct vibration. The Law of Harmony keeps all of them interacting correctly with one another.

You can also see this demonstrated in medical techniques that are using sonic therapy. The vibration of the sound waves will cause a kidney stone to be crushed into much smaller components so that the patient may successfully allow the much smaller components to pass through their urinary system and be released from their body. Sound is a great example of the Law of Vibration. For every sound has its own vibratory essence, and when you find the exact essence in a sound, to do what you wish it to do, it will always act in the same way under the Law of Vibration. Sound, quite literally vibrates to infinity, there is no highest sound or lowest sound. The vibratory patterns of sound are infinite. There are many sounds that you are unable to hear physically.

In very real sense, the vibrations of sound are essential to holding the universe together. What sounds can do to a kidney stone, it could do to the entire universe. The Law of Vibration maintains the vibratory essence of sound to the acceptable limit that the universe can sustain without damage to its integrity.

When one looks at vibrations from a physical standpoint, and one gets into physics and chemistry, the principles involve particles, molecules, then the atoms, the electrons, neutrons, then there is sub-atomic particles. When it all boils down to it, everything is composed of these atoms which are in vibratory harmony, and based on the vibratory rate, number of electrons, neutrons, protons and subatomic particles, it gives that object of element its characteristics, whether its gold, silver, helium, oxygen, nitrogen and etc. Besides these are electrical, charges both positive and negative in the atom and all these are small little universes. Each atom is depicted as a little universe. There are neutrons and protons and then the electrons are whizzing around in their orbits around them.

This is true of every life form, they are composed of these particles.

Let us take you for example. Within your physical being, you are composed of many elements. You must have these elements within you to exist upon earth. The Law of Vibration maintains within your physical body, each of these elements doing exactly what they must do for your body to maintain its integrity. All that is physical eventually ceases to exist in its current physical form. Then the vibration of that life form becomes, again, spiritual.

The act of creation occurs by changing the vibrational rate of the atoms of the universe. You continue to create within your body the elements necessary to maintain your physical structure, and well-being. There is no real mystery here, it is only difficult to put into terms that meet the criteria of being both scientific and metaphysical, but everything is both physical and metaphysical. There are no empty spaces, there are only spaces where nothing can be detected by the means of detection that we currently have available. You are also light, both physically, as well as metaphysically. Were it possible to remove each part of the structure of a human being, science would find that there was still a great deal left that they could not see. That portion is essentially pure light. You are physical, as well as metaphysical light. You are the light of the world. Your own personal light vibrates at its proper rate at all times and under all circumstances. It is light that enables you to see with your physical eye. Lack of light causes humans not to be able to see with their physical eyes, but the light is still there, even if it cannot be seen physically.

It is the Law of Vibration that has your light, or the light of any life form, vibrating at the rate that is correct for you at all times. As you grow spiritually, your light vibrates brighter and brighter, even as the light bulb on an electrical appliance. By increasing the wattage it will increase the degree of light, so as you turn your spiritual rheostat it increases your degree of light. One could somewhat consider that spirit's evolvement is the gradual increase in vibratory rate, so it is much easier for one at a certain vibrational level to be able to drop down their vibrational level than it is to instantly increase it. Spiritual growth evolves through lifetimes. Becoming more spiritually evolved takes time, at a varying rate depending upon the individual efforts. Positive efforts increase the vibrational rate. Obviously all of us have times when we are working our way through challenges and our vibratory level is not at its highest. This is part of the ascension process. At each individual's level of evolvement they have reached a general vibratory level, but there are variations in the level depending upon moods, actions or thinking. In summary, the Law of Vibration states that vibration is the rate of speed at which every life form moves, rotates and maintains its integrity as a form. Thus it maintains the form that is correct for it in its present experience of life. That which is spiritual, is vibrating at a higher or more rapid level that is not visible to the physical eye. Any life form may slow its vibratory rate to become visible. At any time, under extreme emotional spiritual ecstasy, a life form will increase its vibratory rate only to a point that is not damaging to their physical integrity. This, then is the essential of the Law of Vibration. Briefly, this is where love enters in. For it is the Law of Love that maintains all of this with the encouragement to always work towards the highest level of vibratory integrity of spiritual evolvement. Without love, it cannot be done, but then without love nothing can be done.

Universal Spiritual Law of Vibration and Healing

First of all it is important that you know that all healing is vibratory, no matter what else exist. Healing comes from the Law of Vibration which is part of the Law of Love. In medical science healing there are many examples of the use of vibrations to diagnose and heal. To mention a number of these are: Ultra Sounds, Cat Scans (computerized axial tomographic), MRI's (magnetic resonance imaging),cyber-knife, gamma knife and others for surgery. These are very physical manifestation of the Law of Vibration as a necessary tool to the art of healing. In spiritual healing no matter what discipline is undertaken, vibration must be present. The reason for this is that spiritual healing is accomplished by the healer, whether consciously or not, seeking the help of the spirit healers and angelic healers. Spirit life forms have a much more rapid vibration, so when they enter into or come in contact with a physical being or healer, that is calling them to the act of healing, spirit slows their vibratory pattern down sufficient that it might be comfortable for the healer but the healer is also speeding up their vibratory pattern. Thus the vibration of the spirit and the vibration of the physical being come into harmony and the vibration of unconditional love flows from the spirit or the angel, through the healers body into the hands, which are the general tools used in healing both medically and spiritually. Thus the hand is vibrating at a rate that is higher than is normal for a human being. The vibratory energy of healing passes from the healer's hands to whomever they touch. It does not matter if they actually touch the physical body of the person requiring healing or only the aura (Spiritual energy field that surrounds and penetrates the physical body),the healing energy goes directly into and spreads throughout the physical body. The vibration of the healing energy uplifts the physical body and causing the receiver of the energy to vibrate at a higher rate. This stimulates the healing enzymes and all other chemicals within the individuals' body, into a greater activity level. Endorphins are stimulated, adrenalin is stimulated, all of the chemicals in the physical body are stimulated to a higher level of vibrations. It is pure love in action, vibrating through the physical body to create a chemical reaction that will produce only positive healing energy within the body.

This is mediated through the immune and endocrine systems and stimulates other systems of the body that the vibration occurs. This is why if you are watching a spiritual healing, you will often see, even with your physical eyes slight vibration of the healer and slight vibration of the patient. Sometimes the vibration is great indeed. The body may even shake when the energy reaches its maximum power. It is not something that ends as soon as the healer has finished the healing. The energy flow remains a part of the patient and continues to stimulate healing chemicals, immune chemicals, whatever the body needs. It does not even matter where the healers' hands are placed, the energy will go where the energy is needed. It benefits the person being healed mentally, emotionally, spiritually, and physically. Without the Law of Vibration, no healing could occur. It is vital to the healing process. Thus the Law of Vibration is in a very real sense the Law of Healing, without it there is no healing. That is why even persons who are natural channels for the healing energy are wise to have some form of formal education, for their spiritual healing, so they will know how to use the energy they receive, how to maximize it and how to generate it in the most efficient manner. They must also take classes to understand that they are not doing the healing. The healing comes from God, The One, The All. This is very important to understand. It is directed into the physical body from spirit or from angels. The person is not using their own energy to create the healing, they are simply channeling the energy from God. This is why a healer will always feel better after they have done a healing session for some of the enriched, invigorating energy from the vibrational presence of the spirit or angel remains with the healer. Those who understand this never become fatigued from healing. The spiritual healer who believes he or she is doing the healing from their own energy, drains their own personal energy quickly through their self-deception. Spirit works to add to it, but as long as the healer are of the belief that all of this is their energy, they find they are not able to continue with the healing for long periods of time and require rest after a healing. It is important that a healer understands that the Law of Vibration is sharing. They share with you so that you can share with your patient.

Now, on vibratory law in regards to medical healing. Whether they recognize it or not, all healers' hands are healing tools. When surgeons are doing an operation, even before they understand that they were being assisted by spirit, spirit is there to assist them. Their vibratory patterns increased that they might make precisely the right depth of cut, length of cut, to achieve the desired result. They are operating as a channel for the energy of the spirit world to help them in what they are doing. When physicians touch their patient in an examination or medical/surgical procedure or whatever the reason their hands are touching the patient, whether they are conscience of it or not, their hands are healing tools touching their patients in the purest love. When the physician is wearing rubber gloves for hygienic purposes, they do not interfere with the flow of healing energy, that they are receiving and sharing. Every time a physician touches a patient with their hands, with whatever they may be using, the physician, their hands and the instruments becomes one by the Law of Vibration, and they operate within the Law of Vibration, to

Ronald L. Cole, M.D.

bring the best possible result for their patient. This is true of every person who works in any facet of the medical healing profession. They are, whether consciously or subconsciously, a channel for healing and always in touch with the Law of Vibration.

Comments/Examples Law of Vibration

As a note from a scientific stand point, anyone that has studied subjects such as physics or other even basic science courses in high school or college, you are aware that everything that physically exists is composed of electrons, protons and neutrons. These are in a constant and unending state of motion or vibration. If you change the pattern of the motion or vibration you will change the characteristics of the thing you are focused on. This can certainly be an illness or disease process. So whether we change it with medication, radiation or chemotherapy, surgery, and yes even spiritual or emotional energy, we can change the status of the unwanted process of disease. Certainly changing the patients thought process or beliefs by educating them, you can help them "let go" of what negative thoughts they are holding on to and improve their health. I have seen this happen in my medical experience and it is absolutely true and fascinating. Vibrations are a major component in energy itself and loving energy is healing within itself.

I will share a unique experience with you, the reader. Numerous years ago I had invited Rev. Beverly Burdick Carey, my trans-channel medium, to visit me and to do some work together. I had the honor of bringing her into both the operating room and delivery room with me to observe. I was amazed at what she actually saw and observed that she later shared with me. Only a highly evolved and gifted medium is able to see spiritual entities. She saw numerous spiritual entities and most of the entities were busy helping with what was going on. She saw an entity using their hands to assist me with the surgery that I was doing and another was observing and assisting the anesthesiologist. There were personal spiritual guides of the incoming child in the room. The most unique was the operating table. During the surgery and delivery, the angel at the foot of the operating table folded its' wings together and lowered them over the table and the patient in a very loving way. Beverly said it was truly a sight to behold. So we all have a lot of loving help when we ask for it. I know that in over thirty five years I have received much help and protection from the Spiritual realm that I was grateful to receive.

9

UNIVERSAL SPIRITUAL LAW OF FORGIVENESS

The Law of Forgiveness states that forgiveness means to extend to every other aspect of the Consciousness of God, total love and to understand and allow to become unimportant that which has happened which may have caused distress. Forgiveness is one of the most important aspects of the Law of Love. The two are inseparable. Without forgiveness, nothing can be accomplished. Forgiveness then is an active aspect of the Law of Love. Forgiveness is a necessary progression. The Law of Forgiveness, simply stated, means that when something has occurred which has caused a negative result, all parties involved are enabled by their loving progression to forgive themselves for their part in the occurrence, to forgive one another for their part in the occurrence, and to receive the forgiveness of others.

Jesus said it very well, when asked how often one should forgive, he said, "More than once, more than twice, seventy times seventy, and even more", which means that forgiveness must be 100%. There is no limit to the Law of Forgiveness, but there are basic things that control the Law of Forgiveness in its application through human interaction.

The most basic forgiveness is the forgiveness of self. Many humans do things, think things, say things, create things and suffer great guilt for what they have done. They are unable to forgive themselves for their actions, and the consequences of their actions. They, therefore spend sometimes, many lifetimes seeking salvation and not realizing that the first thing they must do is forgive themselves for whatever they have done. Lack of forgiveness is a huge stumbling block to spiritual progression. Guilt and lack of forgiveness, as many things, can extend through and effect a number of lifetimes.

To illustrate, I'll give an example of a very spiritually evolved teacher of mine, Quan Yin. Many thousands of years ago when she was an Atlantian she did certain things with the power of the crystal that were used as the major power source in that empire that resulted in some very wrongful happenings. She did them deliberately, she knew what the results of her actions would be, but she enjoyed the experimentation and the feeling of power that misuse of the crystals gave to her. Her guilt over this in subsequent incarnations was very great, she did not forgive herself. She came into a later incarnation and eventually reached a point in her ministry where she wished to work with crystals, and found she could not do so. Whenever she tried, she was unable to do anything at all. Finally she asked the reason for this seeming inability to do anything at all with crystals even to attend classes where she might learn how to use them. She was shown what she had done, and the consequences, and was told she had failed to forgive herself and release the guilt. She was able then to forgive herself, to release the guilt and to immediately begin her study of and use of crystals, which has certainly aided her ministry and enabled her to help people whom she otherwise would not have been able to help. This is a strong example of the crippling effect of lack of self-forgiveness.

I, therefore recommend that you give yourself a sort of blanket sincere forgiveness for anything you may have thought, said or done at anytime in your present or past. This will free yourself of whatever is holding you back through a lack of forgiveness. Forgiveness is a strong, strong, strong emotion. It is a very freeing emotion. It unleashes much creative power that guilt has kept from being used in its proper form. Refer back to the prayer/affirmation I gave you in a previous chapter.

So the first step in the Law of Forgiveness is self-forgiveness. The second step is other forgiveness. Of course, forgiveness for anything that has happened to you, whether you are aware of it or not is a powerful act of love. Therefore, the Law of Forgiveness in very real ways controls everything you think, say, and do in either a positive, productive, creative way, or in a negative crippling, and non-productive way.

Now, we will take it out of the purely human and personal aspect, and expand it to forgiveness of all things. I will give you a brief example. Supposing one of your animal companions should bite or scratch you. You must forgive the one who did it, because without forgiveness it is impossible to train the companion to the understanding that this is not acceptable behavior. Many persons come to hate certain other life forms when they have been harmed by them. Many people hate, for instances spiders and they perceive them as very nasty life forms, and they will use every means at their command to make certain that that life form does not live very long. This is great un-forgiveness. Inevitably such people are the ones most often bothered by spiders, for they draw to them, by their thought patterns, the very things they do not wish to experience. Thus, the creativity is negative, rather than positive. There is no forgiveness in them. They see spiders as an enemy to be destroyed. If they could begin by forgiving the spider, and seeing this life form as a part of God, a part of themselves, they would cease to interact negatively with the life form, and would cease to be bothered by the life form. I know these sounds odd, but I have personally seen this happen with black widow spiders.

This, of course has some very detrimental effects to human life itself, for often it is discovered at a later date, that a life form has previously been considered poisonous or not very good for the health of humans is found to have very beneficial results in other ways. Foxgloves is an example of this. Foxglove is a very toxic plant with numerous significant side effects and was later found to be a source of digitalis an important heart medication. It was an unforgiven plant for many years in many societies, and yet they are now well known to have very beneficial effects upon the human physique.

There is much to be done to uplift humanity from its unforgiving attitude, into a sense of forgiveness and love. In the Middle East, wars are going on over things that happened centuries ago that the present day participants have not yet forgiven as well as the ingrained prejudices and hatreds that are taught by parents to their children, and the desire to exterminate through a lack of forgiveness all of those perceived to be the ancient and still present enemy.

Before we leave the Law of Forgiveness I would like to briefly bring attention to a very closely related subject and emotion and that is guilt. It is one of the most, if not the most crippling emotions of mankind. It along with fear (and there is not much difference between them) is the most manipulative and devastating emotion that mankind has learned to use against itself and particularly against others. From many sources, people and organizations, man is taught that he is an imperfect and sinful person and he should feel bad and guilty about himself and his deeds. What a perfect way to manipulate people and try to get them to do what others of organizations wants or feels they should do.

If you start early enough in a persons' life when they cannot discriminate about the validity of their training, then it is rather easy to get them to "buy into" the guilt and react to it. Unfortunately, that is what is done, in most societies, ours included. By teaching that you are weak, imperfect, and sinful and that you must change and rid yourself of these traits, since you are a lowly mortal, you will be sentenced to an eternity of damnation if you don't. This mind manipulations occurs on many levels of our society. People are so easily manipulated by guilt and made to feel bad about themselves and their behavior and actions, and this is not necessary. No wonder there is a great need for self, individual, group and national forgiveness. It is not necessary to feel guilty about everything you think, say or do. Just realize you are doing the best you can do under your current set of circumstances and continue to work at individual growth. Remember guilt implies judgement and who has the true right to judge someone. We are all on our own individual path and doing the best we can. Growth is inevitable by any path we choose. Our social philosophy and training should be based on a positive loving approach instead of a negative approach.

No wonder there is such a great need for forgiveness of self and others. Remember, in actuality, there is only one person that can make you feel guilty and that one person is YOU. Others can try to manipulate you by dumping the "guilt trip" on you, but remember, you are the one that either accepts it or rejects it. It is obvious that forgiveness must start with one's self and work outward from there. This is why the Law of Forgiveness is so important. Thus, we go from the pure need to forgive to the universal need to forgive. It must start with each individual, obeying the Law of Forgiveness by first forgiving themselves, then forgiving all others, and allowing that aura of forgiving love to expand forth.

Universal Spiritual Law of Forgiveness and Healing

Without forgiveness it is very difficult to achieve much in a lifetime and particularly it is true of the spiritual area of ones' life. Forgiveness is one of the most powerful energies in the entire universe. The first forgiveness is of oneself. When one forgives oneself, healing occurs often instantly. Most humans walk around with much "baggage" of guilt of not being fully forgiving, thus they are not fully healthy in every possible way. Forgiveness creates immediate result, for forgiveness is a vital vibration of love. When one is self forgiving the healing must follow. When one forgives another, it is a healing act to self and if the other will accept forgiveness, then they are giving themselves a healing through acceptance of forgiveness. If they choose not to allow themselves to be forgiven and say you may forgive me but I cannot forgive myself, then they are denying themselves a portion of the healing that would automatically come if they would say, 'Thank you as you have forgiven me, I also forgive myself." Even if they say it only within, not verbally, the healing vibratory pattern courses through the body, creating healing energy that can not possibly be withheld. For it is by the Law of Forgiveness that healing must occur. It is such a powerful aspect of love, that a very substantial portion of humans who are having difficulty within themselves or within relationships or in obtaining healing, that no matter what they do, have failed to forgive themselves and have frequently failed to forgive others. When the forgiveness is accomplished, the healing must follow. It is the law. It is a setback to every area of life to be unforgiving. It is mentally, emotionally, spiritually and physically crippling to be without forgiveness. In your work and life you must examine yourself most carefully to make certain that you have forgiven yourself for any unloving thought, word or deed and that you have forgiven all who may have caused discomfort to you. For a person to be in a state of total forgiveness, is often difficult, but when achieved, it brings a sense of grace and love into the light which is so uplifting. There are no human words to describe what happens. Examine your subconscious and your conscious mind and examine your soul to make sure you are not harboring any lack of forgiveness of self or any other entity. Heal thyself. Has it not been said, "Physician heal thyself." The first obligation is, unto your own self be true.

Forgiveness of minor things and offenses should not be very difficult, but in this day and time there are many horrific atrocities that occur everyday that is graphically reported on radio, television, the internet and newspapers and magazines which are far more difficult to forgive. Of course, this type of negative activity has been happening and recorded in history for many centuries. I'm not sure I can tell you how you forgive a person who caused great pain, harm and suffering to a family member or close friend. I'm sure it would be very difficult for me as I'm sure it would be for most people.

One important aspect of forgiveness or lack thereof that may help you, is to remember that you can create a great deal of anger, negativity, anguish and pain for yourself as you struggle with forgiveness. As it has been pointed out, this takes a great toll on your happiness, daily life, attitude and your health. You can create a great deal of suffering for yourself, above and beyond what occurred that needs to be forgiven. Doing what is best for your own well being may be your main encouragement.

Time itself may be of assistance in the forgiving process. As is said, "Time heals all wounds", though it is easier said than done. Yes, time does at least help soften emotional or physical trauma if you do not actually hold on to it and keep the "wound" from healing.

I'm not sure why people feel that every major negative incident that occurs must be brought up and relived every year on its anniversary. Of course the news media has a lot to do with this. They have to have something to talk about and sensationalize in highly important "Breaking News" on a daily basis. I'm not saying don't remember friends and loved one's tragedy, but do it in an honorable and loving manner so you don't negatively affect your life or theirs, I'm sure that's how most people would like to be remembered.

You are in full control of how you handle forgiveness. So as with most other things in your life, the more loving you can do it, the more it will help your progress and evolvement as well as be more joyous in your life. Remember you are a part of God, so there is no reason why you should not be forgiven. God does it. The work of forgiveness becomes the responsibility of each individual person. Forgiveness of yourself and others greatly lightens your life's challenges, but the forgiveness must come from the heart and be truly sincere to work its "magic". Remember, you are a part of God and not a born sinner who is condemned to eternal punishment. Forgiveness is indeed a most powerful healer.

10

UNIVERSAL SPIRITUAL LAW OF KARMA

Simply put, the law of Karma is a system of checks and balances. It provides a person with the opportunity to rectify that which has been inappropriately or improperly handled at any time in the past. The law is in effect a joining together of the Laws of Cause and Effect, the Law of Attraction and the Law of Balance. Karma is a equalizing force. Karmically, everything must be brought into balance. Karma simply is what you might call an abbreviation of several laws, and in and of itself demands adherence to the laws it represents. Karma says that whatever is required to put in balance that which is out of balance must and will happen. Karma is the opportunity to experience, to change, to renegotiate that which has happened and to bring it into a state of balance and harmony.

Karma is an aspect of love that is wholly positive, although many people do not recognize this. It is an incorrect belief that if you have misbehaved in the past, you must receive punishment for this. Many think of it in terms of retribution, when in fact it is in terms of balance. Karma helps humans to understand what they have done that was not in the best interest of positive soul growth and evolement. It enables people to obtain information as to ways that they might better enhance the positive growth of the soul. It provides the memory pattern that one needs to make decisions and improvements. It is a universal law because it covers every life form. Mother Earth is as subject to the Law of Karma as you are. Anything that possesses life, consciousness, thought patterns and decision-making abilities is certainly capable of making decisions that are either good for the growth of the soul or not positive for the soul growth. Therefore, it is better to think of karma as the opportunity for positive soul growth than as a means of punishment for prior activities, thoughts, etc. that were not mostly positive.

Let's use the illustration that if one has been a mass murderer in a prior lifetime. By coming in incarnating as a doctor, a minister, a teacher, a social worker, something that is a service to mankind, they may, in one lifetime completely balance that which they created of a negative nature in a prior lifetime. This is of course true, but it is somewhat simplistic. It is a good way to explain in very simple form how karma may work. We need to take it a bit further. We need to ask also if a person has been a mass murderer in a prior lifetime, did not whom he or she murdered also have a part in it. Therefore, we enter into some areas, which are certainly very difficult to understand. They say, no one would wish to be murdered by some crazed psychopath, and yet we understand that there is always cooperation in every endeavor that involves more than one human being. Therefore, the karma becomes not a person karma, but a group karma. All of the individuals involved in that, let us use a round figure, the murderer has murdered ten other humans, we now have eleven people involved in a group karma. We cannot then talk only of what the murderer must do to bring balance to his or her karmic situation, we must also examine what the alleged victims must do to balance their karmic situation. Why would they permit this, what was gained by it, what did they learn as a result of their experience, why did they choose it, what were they attempting to teach the murderer, what were they attempting to teach their loved ones remaining behind upon the earth? What was the murderer trying to learn, what did the murderer teach his or her loved one left behind upon the earth plane? So as you can see, karma is not only a personal thing, it is often a group thing. Even if a person comes in, lives a good and kind life, dies at an advanced age surrounded by loved ones, there is karma existing between that individual, and everyone of his or her acquaintance. There will still be grief at the death of the loved one, a sense of loss. What is to be learned here? We then approach the inevitable fact that the Law of Karma interacts in every single thing we think, say or do. It is a part of our patterns at a highly personal level, and an interactive level.

I know the concept, based on freedom of choice, of each person choosing their time of birth and death, is very difficult for many people in the western world. Also having the responsibility for our life's path and events is also a reality most people question. Both of these concepts are somewhat contrary to what has been taught for generations. Don't get bogged down with these concepts here, just for now understand that LOVE AND FORGIVENESS ARE THE KEY FACTORS FOR BALANCING KARMA. I will discuss these two major and important principles in more detail in my next book. Fortunately with the Law of Love being the primary law, karma can be kept in balance mainly through being a loving individual and attempting to learn unconditional love for everything and everyone. This will certainly increase the positive karmic emanation and vibration of an individual, provide a valuable teaching experience for those who are associated with this individual, and encourage more and more people into more and more loving interactions with themselves and other individuals. It is frequently valuable for an individual to seek out some understanding of their karmic connection with one another, and certainly, of whatever you would call negative karma they are carrying. It is not sufficient only to understand, for you must still balance the karma. It would therefore be correct to say that if a given individual were to love unconditionally every person with whom they came into contact with and loved themselves unconditionally, their karma would rapidly come into a state of perfect balance and remain in that perfectly balanced state as long as they continue unconditional love. It is however, equally correct to say that this is not a common happening. Therefore the universal law allows for what could best be described as small increments of karmic balance in each lifetime. A person should attempt to achieve unconditional love with as many individuals as possible, knowing that each time you achieve unconditional love with a given individual their karma is that much clearer and closer to balance. There are very few individuals who return to spirit realms without having expressed and experienced unconditional love for a least one other individual. Thus it may be a slow process of achieving perfect karmic balance, but it is a process that everyone eventually concludes. For most people, the way the karma law affects them and the actual total balance is a gradual thing through many lifetimes as well as the time spent in spirit realms between physical life expression. Eventually a point is reached in one's spiritual evolvement where there is an almost sudden knowing that that individual truly loves everyone and everything without any conditions. Of course this is not easy to do and takes time and effort, but the rewards are great. This provides a release of the other emotions that binds people together such as the emotions of expectations, jealousy and envy. These are powerful ties in human behavior, as are many other less than loving emotions. When their lesser emotions are replaced with unconditional love then, as was Jesus, Buddha and others, one has achieved the Christhood, and one is only capable of unconditional love.

A recognition and understanding is achieved the moment absolute and unconditional love is achieved, Christhood is thus achieved and once achieved it can never be unachieved. For that moment, the unconditional Universal Law of Love takes place, is a moment of permanent change. Just as when an egg and a sperm unite, it is an instant of permanent change, they cannot ever again be an egg and a sperm, they will go on to be a human being. At the instant of conception two individual life forms have united to produce a human being or whatever the ovum and the sperm are meant to be. With achieving Christhood, it is total mental, emotional and spiritual establishment and never again is that individual less than a Christ. We all have work yet to do to reach this level or we would not be in this physical body.

It is often said that we are a part of Christ. This is true in that the potentiality of Christhood exists in everyone, and that is all part of the Universal Law of Karma that has helped the individual to make the choices that will achieve perfect karmic balance. How many lifetimes are required? Only one is actually required, but it is very doubtful that it has ever happened to any individual in a single incarnation. The required number is as many as it takes, for there is no time limit, there is only eternity. In the human conception of time, every physical body will eventually cease to exist as a viable physical body, that matters not, for the atoms that compose the physical body are redistributed to other physical bodies. The entire solar system, galaxy and universe will cease to exist physically and life and the atoms that have made up the universe are constantly being recycled into other physical forms of life. Physical life itself does not cease to exist only a certain form of physical life. Mother Earth or "Gaia" loves her children. She has achieved the ability to love all of the life forms that inhabit her without any conditions, she simply loves. Therefore in a very real sense Gaia is a Christ, but not all of her life forms have achieved Christhood.

The power of prayer reached a point where enough human beings upon the planet were working towards peace, love and enlightenment. Daily gathering in groups to pray for peace and individual daily prayers were adequate that the consciousness of humanity, without most humans being aware of it, shifted just enough to remove from human consciousness the possibility of using the weapons of mass destruction to destroy Mother Earth. When this happened, the consciousness of Gaia also shifted, for her consciousness is interactive with the life form that lives upon her. Now through the Karmic Law, Balance (presented later) and Cause and Effect we live upon a planet, which is a Christ. The cause of the Christhood was the shift in human consciousness that provided that moment of unconditional love that created a Christ planet. It is good to know that while in parliamentary procedures the majority rules, in spiritual procedure a loving minority may well rule over a less than loving majority, for indeed those who pray and work are not in the majority. But so great is the power of love, the power of prayer and the power of desire for peace, and tranquility, that prayers of the minority were sufficient to create that shifting of human consciousness. Prayer is the single most powerful thought form in the universe. The power of prayer and love is truly great. More will be discussed about prayer when the Law of Prayer, Meditation and Thought is presented.

Many people believe karma means or indicates that one must pay "an eye for an eye". They define trying to balance karma in a negative way. If someone did something "bad" or injurious to you, then they have to have you injure them in return in order to have your karma balanced. Let's examine this in more detail.

It became the understanding of people that retribution and karma were interchangeable through human observation of human activity. For instance, if George hit Peter, and Peter hit George back, through human sensitivities this action was balanced. As people began to examine beyond what they could see with their own eyes, they created their own law of karma, which followed their examination of physical behavior. Now, the observance came that sometime George hit Peter, and before Peter could return the favor, George was dead. Therefore, George escaped the retribution he should have received at the hands of Peter. How to accomplish balance? George and Peter may come back again and Peter may hit George. Many humans have always believed in reincarnation. Few human cultures have not believed that you will come back again. Thus, the idea became associated with, perhaps the reason that we incarnate is so that we can bring this balance about. If I am very good in this lifetime and I hurt no one, then I may come back again, and be very highly thought of and no one will hurt me. But if I am bad, and hurt others, then everyone of them will seek to hurt me. This is a simplistic explanation, but it is not accurate or valid. Thus, the whole Law of Karma became, at that point, a human invention, having nothing to do with the divine universal aspect of karma. It makes sense to humans, that very bad people should be punished. If they could not punish them, it gave comfort to believe that somewhere along the lines of incarnation they would certainly be punished. Then, religions entered in and religions are created or propagated by humans. The negative aspect, and miscreation concerning karma became a part of dogma of many religions and was carried to huge extremes.

Eventually, this belief of "an eye for an eye" became so popular because it presented suffering human beings with the comfort that the one who made them suffer would certainly pay, if not in this lifetime, in another lifetime. Now, with this huge amount of mass consciousness acting on this negative definition of karma, people at a very early age were influenced with this false belief and followed it. This perpetuated the negativity or incorrect belief. It became law to societies, but fortunately human law does not govern divine law. Now in comparatively recent times, only within the past perhaps one hundred years has the true positive Law of Karma been taught. Certainly, in recent years more and more teachers are beginning to understand that karma means balancing love, not retribution in time. Eventually, of course, the majority of people will recognize this and then indeed will the great and glorious and loving Law of Karma influence the consciousness of humans towards the light. As they understand, they need not suffer. They will create for themselves glorious, loving lives, free of the enslavement they themselves created through believing that retribution was the law of God.

So we see the Law of Karma, like all other universal laws is tied in closely with love. Negativity does not have to be balanced by added negativity, but it can simply be transmuted or erased with love and forgiveness. Again, unconditional love is the ultimate transmuter, eraser, healer, balance and energy form that exists. One only elevates themselves to a higher spiritual level of evolvement and existence with the practice of love and not believing "an eye for an eye". One can instantly wipe out, or balance karma by a simple act of true unconditional love. Absolutely no retribution is required. In fact, retribution does not balance karma, but perpetuates its cycle and can for many lifetimes. This is not necessary, unless the true knowledge and lesson of karma and love is not learned or is ignored.

When more and more people learn the true positive meaning of karma and practice it, this world will rapidly become a better place built on love and not retribution.

One last example of negative karma that is and has been very obvious today, is the continued ethnic fighting and wars that are occurring in the Middle East and Europe. Very young children are taught hate and violence before they can be discriminating with their thought. They are like young "non-screening" sponges that soak up the hatred and need for retribution before they have the chance to learn the unlimited power of love. Therefore, every day, we see scenes of the results of this negative programming on our television sets and in printed and electronic news. These wars and hatred have gone on so long most people can't even remember its' true origin. And in truth, the simple common man on each side still probably wants the same thing. That is to simply live their life in peace and amply provide for himself and his family. But the mass consciousness of hatred and reaction perpetuates the senseless suffering and loss of life. Again, negative karma can simply be erased and balanced with love and forgiveness. We should all strive for this.

Universal Spiritual Law of Karma and Healing

The Law of Karma is quite simply, a law of bringing things into balance through love. Since love is the great creative force of the universe, it makes sense in healing to examine relationships with others to find out if the karma the two of you share is any way out of balance. If it is, we bring the Law of Forgiveness and we balance the karma through love and create healing. Balanced karma is a healing energy, unbalanced karma may bring distress, discomfort and disease to humans, for it is accompanied by guilt, which is of course an energy of destruction rather than construction. Karma must be seen for what it is, a way to evaluate the balance of your entire life. Many people fear karma but it is simply a means by which one evaluates that which has been, so they may plan for that which will be. Karma is a word that people have given great destructive powers to, but it is in fact a constructive thing for it enables an individual to use the Laws of Love, Balance, etc. to make themselves a healthier individual. Each person has thought, said or done things which are not positive and loving. The karma is certainly out of adjustment because of this, but that can be readily brought back into balance by the simple act of forgiving ones' self, forgiving all others, and asking that any negative thought, words or deeds that have ever been manifested be transmuted by love to perfect and loving energy. Karma is a reminder that we have the obligation and responsibility to forgive and love.

I therefore recommend that each day you practice an act of forgiveness by using the prayers and affirmation I gave you in a previous chapter. They are powerful and help cleans you on a day to day basis. Along with the prayers you should learn from your less than loving thoughts, words and deeds and act in more loving ways to yourself and all other manifestations of God. This helps further your spiritual evolvement and balance Karma.

So as mentioned above, most people look at Karma as a negative "pay back" system that often requires suffering to balance. If people feel that way, they begin to believe suffering, illness or disease are required and therefore create these conditions in their life. They do not understand the true power of love and forgiveness in having a truly balanced and healthy life. God wants us to learn and evolve from our "mistakes", but you must do this truly from your heart.

To summarize the healing aspects of the Law of Karma, they are essentially the same thing. They are both a balance of your past thoughts, words and deeds (karma) and that balance creates the balance or imbalance of the physical functioning and well-being of your body and health. It is healing in action. Positive karma promotes healing whereas negative karma promotes illness and disease. This simply says, you control your healing process and as stated before, like most things it all boils down to love.

UNIVERSAL SPIRITUAL LAW OF MULTIPLICATION

The Law of Multiplication states that all things, physical and non-physical, multiply, nothing is static. All things are in movement, action and in multiplication. The universe by it's own divine laws must multiply, must continue to grow and must reproduce itself. Therefore, the Law of Multiplication makes certain that all things, from the infinitesimal to the infinite do reproduce and multiply themselves, becoming more than they were before. Nothing is ever diminished, everything is an active growth pattern under the Law of Multiplication.

It is natural for everything to multiply itself. The need for self-replication falls under the Law of Multiplication of substance. Each tree produces hundreds of thousands of seeds, according to the kind of tree that it is. One tiny seed planted in the ground grows to a stalk of wheat which produces hundreds of seeds. Infants are conceived in every life form through the multiplication of substance. It is natural, then for everything to not only reproduce itself, procreate itself, but multiply itself. The joining of the egg and ovum of a human couple produces a child with billions of cells, beginning with two cells. All things then, naturally multiply themselves, then continue doing so as long as the terms and needs of their particular species are met. It is under these laws then that one should think in terms of how to multiply the other aspects of life.

It is important to understand that the Law of Multiplication applies to all aspects of life, physically, emotionally, and spiritually. So, this is why it is, for each human being, each human family, and each human clan or group to decide what they want to multiply in their lives. Whatever you have in your life now is what you have chosen to multiply. This would include such physical things as home, appliances, automobiles, money, bank account, investments, numbers of children in the family, and such metaphysical things as joy, peace love, harmony, interaction and of course the opposite of these things. A family which exist in misery continues to multiply that misery, and it becomes a generational thing. Families, which are working in the essence of joy, multiply these emotions, feelings, and metaphysical substances in their family life. One must seek guidance from the inner self, from the spirit being, from the Godself, and decide what do I want in my life, what do I want to multiply for me and those around me. When you have set the goal for your life, the natural process of multiplication takes over.

You have met in your life, people who seem to maintain an optimistic and joyous attitude towards life, even when they are going through a difficult period in their life. They know they will succeed, they will come through, they will be happy and positive again, even though they may not be in the moment, and so they are. Conversely, you have met people who only see the negative in everything. All of life is gray and dismal, they can find no joy in anything. Consequently, they continue to become more and more miserable unhappy, sick, and frequently die at a relatively early age, from the massive amounts of negative thinking that they are projecting and multiplying. The person who always complains and is unhappy will be the one with the most health problems.

Your beliefs and attitudes are the key to your well-being. So keep them positive and let go of the negative. So no matter what your thoughts, visions, goals and actions are, the multiplication goes on. If you always keep in mind that everything you think, say or do will multiply itself, then you will be able to concentrate your thoughts, words and deeds in the areas that you truly wish them to go.

For instance, a loving word, glance or act multiplies itself. When you share love, you draw love to you, which gives you more love to share. When a person is angry and ugly to those around him or her, they draw only misery to themselves. Everything multiples. Psychology teaches that a child that is severely abused, and mistreated in it's formative years may well grow up to be an abusive parent. This is often true. What happens, multiplies itself. Your good thoughts multiply themselves and go forth into the etheric waves to create more love and evil thoughts multiply the same way. Those who truly understand the Law of Multiplication of substance, or at least as much as anyone is capable of understanding it, make certain that their thoughts were indeed of a positive and loving nature, knowing that whatever they are doing will multiply itself.

Money also multiplies itself, and perhaps from the human point of view this is one of the most important things to recognize, money creates money. Since money is the energy form that most humans are currently using to make things happen and to create things, it must be wisely invested and wisely used, that it continues to multiply itself. The person who hordes their money in a tin can, and buries it in the back yard will certainly have as much as they had, but no more. I would never advise that it simply be hidden and locked away. It does not do the miser any good, and it does not multiply itself magically in a box. Those who are aware of the Law of Multiplication of substance in the affairs of their financial portions of life invest wisely and find that the money multiplies itself. Farmers, knowing well the multiplication of substance, plant their seeds and expect that a great crop will emerge given proper growing conditions. Great companies invest their resources in research and development, knowing that what they are spending in this area will multiply their profits in time to come. So, although not all people understand the multiplication of substance, they know it and they use it.

It would be wise to begin each day when you are able to, asking what do I wish to accomplish this day, and how will it multiply itself in my life. If you give yourself, but one goal, for instance, today I will spend an extra hour with my children in the garden, just enjoying quiet and company, this will multiply itself in many ways, one of which is that your children will remember such times as they grow to adulthood. It will help them to be better parents should they choose to marry and have children. Today, for instance you could take your wife out to dinner, just the two of you and you will multiply the love and companionship between the two of you. One might say, today I will give myself a break, and enjoy my own company for half of an hour and this will multiply your understanding of yourself in your professional life also. There are many ways to multiply, and you can continue to find other ways.

Let's look at an example of say, someone in your work place has wronged you unjustly or tried to damage your reputation and you felt you should seek the assistance of an attorney to protect yourself from this unjust action. To see an attorney is in a sense multiplication. You are accomplishing, by this, several needed goals, which in time will multiply themselves. You are accomplishing the return of your cash outlay for say attorney's fees that you should never had to expend, and you can take the money or a portion of it and use it to pay current bills, or whatever you wish to do. It is energy of which you have available to use whenever it is returned to you.

You are multiplying your own sense of bringing things back into balance again. This situation has seriously impeded your professional and personal sense of balance. How could it not? You are providing an opportunity for other less kind co-workers to rethink their attitudes and actions and perhaps in the future to make wiser decisions. Thus, multiplying wisdom, discretion, etc. in the area in which you work and among the people with whom you work. You are at least providing an opportunity for multiplication in these areas. Whether your co-workers choose to accept this opportunity for growth is, of course, no consideration of yours. You will give the growth opportunity to them. If they do not wish to multiply their own character in a positive direction, then you at least have done what you are supposed to do, which is provide them with the opportunity. On the other hand, your own strength of character will be multiplied by knowing that what you have done is best for all concerned. You will feel a greater strength of character, a greater sense of righteousness, a greater sense of balance, so in everything that you do, everything that you think and everything that you say, know the Law of Multiplication is working. It is up to each individual to make certain they are working for positive multiplication and gain, since as thoughts, words and deeds that you "send out" will often come back to you in multiplied form.

Universal Spiritual Law of Multiplication and Healing

All things by their nature multiply themselves constantly. As you read, your body is multiplying itself. It is releasing that which it no longer needs and replacing it with things that are necessary such as the necessary hormones, enzymes and immune energies. The Law of Multiplication, shows that nothing has limits. Since nothing has limits, multiplication naturally, when properly used, is a healing energy for it multiplies those things which creates healing energy within the physical body. At the same time, removes that which does not by simple supplanting it. Even as two times two equals four, will be supplanted by four times four equals sixteen. The law of multiplication is a powerful healing energy when humans realize it multiplies that which is needed and replaces that which is not. In this wonderful experimentation through the Law of Multiplication, healing naturally occurs. Thus one can observe one's physical body and watch the process. It can be physically seen when a person cuts themselves. They have separated skin, fat and muscle to whatever the degree the cut exists, but the healing forces of multiplication immediately go into action multiplying quickly the healing energy required.to heal the wound and eventually make it disappear. When one observed their own bodily process of multiplication it is easy to understand how the same process is healing within the body where one cannot physically see. Thus this Law of Multiplication is part of the entire process of healing, multiplying that which is necessary and replacing that which is no longer necessary. Multiplication is an ongoing process in the physical body and it is designated to healing. What is not understood is that the multiplication may take a form that seems distressing to the physical body, but that can quickly be eliminated by positive thought which multiplies the action of the beneficial chemicals and energy in the physical body bringing, of course, healing. Thus multiplication as with every universal law is part of the healing process.

12

UNIVERSAL SPIRITUAL LAW OF ATTUNEMENT

The law of Attunement indicates that without things being attuned to one another, they would "fall apart". It is an active law that keeps everything where it belongs, doing what it should and tuned to every other thing. Simply put, attunement is awareness of everything in the universe. For example, when you tune up a car, you make everything work in reference to everything else, and that is the Universal Law of Attunement. Nothing is created in the universe that does not work with every other thing. This law is a part of the healing aspect that keeps things attuned to one another, aware of one another and constantly in adjustment to one another.

The Law of Attunement, and the Law of Karma are closely intertwined. Everything in the universe is in attunement with everything else when all things are in their state of perfection, which can only happen when everything is moving karmically in the direction that it must go. Karma is a powerful law. Attunement can also be described as when a musician tunes their instrument so that each note is perfect. The universe is an instrument of perfection. When all are operating in perfect attunement, the literal music of the universe is perfect.

The Law of Attunement gives to each portion of the universe its own note. Humans are capable of hearing many musical sounds, however no one is capable of hearing all of the musical sounds the universe offers. It is very hard for some people to understand that every manifest portion of God resonates in attunement with every other portion, and that each portion has its own specific note. Humans are delineated by the notes they are capable of hearing, and it goes well beyond that. You have your own special note in the universe. It is not the same as any other note of any human or any life form or any planet. It is yours and yours alone. It is part of your karma. Those who are able to psychically hear the perfect note of each individual, can tell immediately whether that individual is in attunement or not, can tell the condition of the karma of that individual and know the soul's progression of that individual. Under the Law of Attunement that note will only strike perfectly if everything is in perfect order, and if all karma is in balance. Needless to say, such psychic beings rarely encounter a perfect note.

Although the note may not be perfect, it may still be pleasant to hear. For indeed, although you may find this difficult to believe or understand, there are truly very few beings of any kind in the universe who are so badly out of balance that their note is actually painful. These are encountered from time to time.

Let me give you an example. Our sociologists estimate that less than 10% of all human beings in the United States commit crimes of violence or indeed crimes of any kind, and yet if one pays only attention to their newspapers, and newscasts upon radio and television one would quickly believe that everybody is busily engaged in violent acts of crime. This is a false picture. So, it is throughout the universe, those whose karma is so badly unbalanced that their karmic note, their note of attunement, is actually disturbing to hear are less than 10% of all living beings. At the other end of the scale, less the 10% of all physical beings in the universe are so attuned that the psychic ear will hear a perfect note. The vast majority of physical life forms have a note that is obviously not yet perfect, but is certainly not distressing to hear.

Now, in the spirit world, and the angelic world, and other non-physical worlds the proportion of deeply disturbing notes of attunement is even less, and the proportion of perfect notes of attunement is higher, but still the vast majority of spirit beings are not yet perfected. Otherwise, we would not need to keep working. Remember that there is no end to spiritual progression and we are all evolving as well as the great spiritual masters.

Even though we are always working on spiritual progression, we can come so much into attunement that while we continue progression, the note is perfect. Remember, that different life forms also have their effect upon the attunement. Although the note remains the same, there may be times when momentarily a note is perfect, but then persons are doing other things that could put it out of attunement. All of this is in conjunction with karma, for everything you do, has its effects upon your karma and the balance of your karma and thus affects your attunement. Thus, keep in mind each thought you have, each word you speak, each deed you commit has its effect upon your note in the Law of Attunement, therefore strive to keep harmony and balance so that your note will be beautiful and perfect. That is the Law of Attunement.

Ronald L. Cole, M.D.

Universal Spiritual Law of Attunement and Healing

The Law of Attunement brings each thing into perfect attunement and Oneness with everything else. All of the physical body is naturally attuned to all other parts of the body. All of the physical body is attune to the spiritual essences of life. In a perfectly attuned body there is of course, no disease, distress or discomfort. When a body is not attuned, the energies do not flow harmoniously with one another, thus causing disease, distress and disharmony. When one is working with the Law of Attunement one envisions the physical body with every single portion of itself, down to the tiniest molecular structure, as being in perfect attunement working flawlessly together. Respect is there for the great and glorious creation of a physical body. Respect of oneself is one of the ways in which the body is placed in attunement, again loving and forgiving oneself. The Law of Attunement helps to keep all of the bodily functions in tuned with one another, that the body might function perfectly. If it is not functioning perfectly, something is not attuned to something else. As soon as the attunement takes place the healing is accomplished. It may not occur instantaneous, but it will most certainly occur. All of these things of which we have spoken are dependent, of course, upon the Law of Love, whose axiom is love yourself for you are God. Healing then is accomplished through all of these things. Without the Law of Attunement the body would not be in a state of harmony with itself. Most infants are born in perfect harmony with themselves. Exposure to non-positive vibrations upon entering the physical world may cause a dis-attunement in the infant which must then be treated. When you begin to feel a sickness come upon you, seek for what part of your mind, emotion, spirit or physical being is not in a total attunement. All must be attuned to enter into that perfect state of One which knows without question, it is God.

I know it is easy to say to seek what part of you is not in total attunement, but in many cases of illness, disease and distress it is not easy to determine what is not in attunement or balance and simply readjust it and be healed. The biggest reason this is difficult is that we have not been taught the real truths of life, both physical and spiritual and over many centuries we were not taught that the true bottom cause of health is our thoughts, words and deeds and our accepted belief systems. We have spent many lifetimes of accepting that ill-health comes from physical causes. Again, the physical causes that fill medical libraries are only the mechanisms that manifests the disease processes which originated from our internal dys-ease and not applying Universal Spiritual Laws in a positive manner both physically and spiritually.

UNIVERSAL SPIRITUAL LAW OF JOY

13

This law states that because all things are already perfect, because all things are constantly multiplying, because life is an infinite thing, joy is the natural character of all creation. Joy is the law that says look at me and be happy. I am perfect, we are perfect, all is perfect. Without joy, nothings can be created, nothing could happen. Joy is a law that governs the consciousness of every aspect of creation. Joy is not only governing, it is a reactive thing, because of how perfect joy is, it is seen as profoundly creative, reactive and sensitive to everything that is of the universe.

The Universal Law of Joy states emphatically, and without exception, that the perfect will of God is that all aspects of the Conscious of God should know nothing but joy at all times. What is joy? Joy is an all encompassing sense of peace, harmony, elation, laughter, optimism, delight in all things and an outpouring of love and intaking of love. Joy holds within itself all that is loving, good, beautiful, fun, uplifting and outreaching that you can possibly imagine, and much that you cannot imagine. Joy to the world is the Law of God, it is not merely a song that is sung at certain times of the Christian year. It is a law, it is in effect at all times. God is that which is within everything that is. God is physical in the sense that God manifests physically in humans, animals, plants, minerals, planets, stars and life forms you cannot even imagine. Joy to the world, for the world is God, and God is the purest kind of joy. The permissive will of God permits God's affect to feel anything It chooses to experience and to create anything It chooses to. Sometimes that which is experienced, is joy and sometimes it is not. The Law of Joy is perhaps the simplest, at the same time, one of the most profound of God's laws.

Think of times when you have felt nothing but absolute joy. This is how you are suppose to feel all the time. Interference with the Law of Joy is a decision that is made by life forms called learning experiences, and sometimes they are less than joyous. If you will remember, that joy to the world, is the Law of God, then you can find joy in all things because the world is God. Again we've come back to the optimist and the pessimist. Essentially an optimist is one who can find the good and thus the joy in all things. A pessimist is one who has given up on their being good, and can always find the negative, and the unhappy. For some people, this is a necessary part of growth, they do not know how else to grow, but a choice is always available. Joy is a natural thing, it is easier to laugh than to cry, it is easier and healthier for the face to smile than to frown. This proves that joy is natural, and agony unnatural. Joy in its coexistence with the Law of Multiplication, for instance, multiplies itself. When people are happy, they tend to continue to be happy because they prefer it to being unhappy. When people are laughing, they tend to continue to find things so that they will laugh more, because it feels good. When people are experiencing beauty in their lives, they tend to want more, so that they can continue the joyous appreciation of that which is beautiful. Joy, like all things, is self-replicating. Like all laws of God, you have the choice as to whether you wish to follow it or not.

When you are in the Law of Joy you may see the things that are less joyous and wish to change them to greater joy, but you will not allow yourself to become depressed and un-joyous. For instance it is hard to see suffering of children in the world. It is dreadful to think that numerous children are used and miserable, but to allow one's self to become so overwhelmed by what is happening that all you do is dwell upon it, does not create any cure for it. It only makes a person more miserable. To look upon the situation, such as the mistreatment of the children, as an evil to be changed, and to then joyously enter in some positive action designed to help children is more effective. It is impossible to estimate how many humans upon the planet truly suffer because of the negativity they see around them, but their suffering prevents them from doing anything to alleviate it. If they can enter into the Law of Joy, they can admit that there are things that are wrong, they can find a way to help make them better and right. Without joy, positive creativity is very difficult and for many people impossible. The medical profession must finally come to recognize this, and fortunately certain doctors are writing books, such as "Laughter is Good Medicine". They are encouraging an optimistic and joyous attitude in their patients, and in the persons who are working with the patients. They are encouraging laughter and joy and smiling, and it works. Of course it works, joy is a tremendous healer. The very emotion of joy creates an instantaneous healing activity, which if continued, could heal all things. Joy is one of the most healing of emotions. As an example, many are so distressed over various areas of the world that are at war, killing and genocide. There is much distress and no joy, and people say, "But how can I be joyous when I think of my brothers and sisters being killed." No, you cannot feel joy in this, but you can take joy in the thought that there are things you can do to alleviate these situations, and once you begin this positive thinking, the energy, the joy, it creates within you will bring about ideas, plans and thought patterns that may be very helpful and uplifting to human consciousness, to where it no longer desires to kill that which is different.

Without joy, nothing good can be imagined, created, substantiated, or in existence. The Law of Joy is truly one of the greatest aspects of the Law of Love. Joy and love are virtually interchangeable words, for we find that the more people love, the more capable they are of experiencing true joy. I do not mean by this the feeling of gaiety and hilarity that is an aspect of human emotion, when things are in a happy state and going well. Joy is a deep sense of contentment, optimism, recognition of one's place in the universe, one's unity with the God Force, knowing one's self to be a part of God and knowing God is all there is. Joy is a natural feeling, a natural knowing and a natural condition in which to be. To be otherwise is abnormal and out of sync with the Law of Love. There is a song that is sung at the time of Christmas, Joy to the World. This should be sung everyday. It is a proclamation, it is a prayer and it is an affirmation. Joy is to the world, it is of the world and a natural state of being. It is not a fleeting effervescent thing. It is a deep inward sense.

When one has evolved to a state of cosmic consciousness, the quotient of joy in their inner being is dramatically increased, for no matter what may be happening in the physical life, what may seem to be interfering with the harmony of life, there is the ever-present, deep knowing that God is all there is, and this is where the joy comes from. We find that persons who are in cosmic consciousness, and in that state of Oneness with God, may experience times when things in their life are certainly not as they want them to be, when they are going through challenging times. The joy creates in them the confidence to know beyond any question of doubt that they are at One with God, and therefore the things they are experiencing, they will master. It enables a cosmically conscious individual to see everything as a learning experience, an opportunity for mental, emotional, spiritual and physical growth. It enables the person to look at life's challenges as learning opportunities, rather than an obstacle in the pathway toward a desired goal. It reduces the depression that seems to take over people from time to time. There will be times when there is not hilarity and gaiety in one's life, but the inner knowing keeps the joy energy always there, and because of that energy of joy, the person is enabled to think more clearly, to be more creative and to find ways to master the challenge, which the individual is facing. They do not ever become completely depressed and unable to function, or unable to see a way out of the current thought process.

Therefore, the Law of Joy is essential to the creative process of life itself. It is not restricted, of course to humans. We have many non-human companions sharing our lives and homes. You can observe in them their natural sense of joy because they do not reason and think in the same way that humans do, because they tend to live in the moment. They are not oppressed by the things that oppress humans. They remain joyous, and they show their joy. For instance, your non-human family members respond to the presence of one another and to the presence of humans whose homes they share. They show their joy in the interaction. They are not concerned that perhaps one of their members will not come home, they are joyous when you come home.

It is easy for humans to say that my cat, dog or parakeet does not have to provide its own food and shelter. This is true for the domestic animals. Even animals in the wild live in the moment, they search to fulfill their needs. Their basic personality is to go for what they need, to acquire it, to enjoy it and not to worry about tomorrow. Therefore, non-human life forms may have a higher knowledge of, and living within the Law of Joy. Humans tend to project the negative thoughts of today into activities of tomorrow, thus diminishing their joy in today. Learning to live, appreciating the things that are uplifting today, and confidently expecting that whatever opportunity presents itself in the days to come will be in your behalf, can help you to remain more joyous. Humans often think of joy as an effervescent feeling, that they either have or do not have. They are joyous when things are going right, and they are not when things are not going right. That is an entirely untrue concept. When a person has accepted joy in its true spiritual form into their life, it is always there. It is the spark that helps to maintain optimism and it is the energy that provides creative thought to achieve the desired goals. It is the essence of drawing together humans in every kind of interpersonal relationship. It is a lack of joy that creates family disharmony, national disharmony and international disharmony. Persons who do not understand the Law of Joy are prone to find things always negative. They tend to see the bad in things, and react, of course to what they perceive to be the negative. Those who have the quality of joy as a part of their whole personality, character and lifestyle, may recognize and indeed effectively deal with things that are less than perfect. Always, they have that sense of optimism that something can be done, that a solution is there and that they will create it, find it, use it and benefit from it. One of the most meaningful and profound sayings that was given me years ago at a time of distress that means a great deal to me was TRUST ALL JOY. It carries great meaning and comfort. Think about it and your own joyful experiences.

Let us look at an examples of how joy and equality of love, influences human decisions. Let us take a rather common occurrence in human interactions. Two persons meet, find one another attractive, begin the process of falling in love, and perhaps deciding to spend their life together. In the process, great joy is experienced, each individual sees in the other an object of admiration, passion and qualities that are mutually desirable. In this early stage of falling in love, persons often say, "Everything seems so wonderful, happy, and I am full of joy". They feel confident, all of their senses are maximized and everything seems perfect. This is a stunning example of the quality of joy in action. This primary stage of the business of falling in love is joy in action.

This high state of joy does not maintain, could not maintain, for people are not so constructive that they can exist perpetually in a state of emotional high with all of their senses inundated. Eventually the senses become overloaded, and the sense of reality steps in. This is when the love either begins to mature into something enduring, or is recognized as what we term infatuation. When it translates or transmutes into a deeper love, the joy is not as keenly felt, but it is still there. There is comfort in looking at a beloved face across the dinner table at night. There is comfort in knowing that you will share your home and share your lifestyle. You may not look at each other constantly with admiration, but you look at each other with a sense of inner comfort, knowing that the love is a joyous thing. It still brings happiness to you. True joy is the inner sense of comfort and confidence that a happy and successful relationship has, not the hyper-extended euphoria of the infatuation period that is necessary to bring two people together, but the joy of love shared is truly the cement that holds the relationship together. When that joy is a natural part of life, through cosmic consciousness, all things seem possible, and indeed all things are possible. Those who are without that inner security are without a rudder, for joy is the rudder on the ship of love, so to speak, the guidance, the direction. That which persons enjoy, they seek to continue doing. That which they do not, they will eventually cease to do. Reach for it in all decision making, reach for it when things seem to be going in a way contrary to your needs and desires. Reach within, find that confidence, that element of joy, trust it, it is permanently there. It is a part of you and it can be trusted as stated above.

Another aspect of the Law of Joy is that it allows one to not limit their options, and creative power. Most people decide that they wish to have something resolved in a certain way, and they go towards that resolution, without truly examining every possible option. Those who have the quality of joy will examine options that others would not even think of examining, because they are lacking in the creative ability that the Law of Joy offers to them. They have chosen not to accept this limitless opportunity, while those with joy in their heart will accept it. Those who keep joy active in their life will find themselves more in balance and a sense of inner-calmness which helps them handle the daily challenges of life.

An important point is that joy and happiness are not the same thing. Happiness is a feeling or emotion that is not permanent, where as joy, when it is achieved, is an essence that is permanent. So you see, joy is a very important law and essence, so you and others greatly benefit by bringing joy to yourself, others and the world. Remember: Trust All Joy.

Universal Spiritual law of Joy and Healing

The Universal Law of Joy is an open and generous outpouring of love. Honest unconditional love for oneself and for others around and about them and for situations that exist by its very nature. Joy causes things to happen within the mental, emotional, spiritual and physical aspects of the individual by experiencing feelings of joy. Feelings of joy causes face muscles to be used in smiles, in laughter, in sound that causes other people to join in. A smile is infectious, laughter is infectious, so thus the person first experiencing joy creates a chain reaction in which everyone participates. This feeling, this usage of muscles, this enjoyable sound causes healing energy to be activated within the physical body. This is something that medical science is aware of now, that happier people, more joyous people, typically have fewer physical afflictions and what they do suffer from, is more readily treated, handled, and cured. Joy creates chemicals within the body that are beneficial to the body's good health and longevity. Happy people, generally speaking, live longer then do unhappy people. Joy then is a powerful emotion that creates highly effective antibodies, anti-viral chemicals, chemicals that uplift unhappiness and depression and chemicals that create a stable balance within an individual that produces the necessary chemicals in the physical body to initiate healing and continue the healing.

Those persons who are depressed and unhappy are not producing the chemicals that joyous conditions produce. Thus the body does suffer physically when depression is part of the character or personality of an individual. The production of destructive chemicals causes the body to become ill and it becomes incapable of fighting off the illnesses. When joy is restored so that the body may take up the production of healing chemicals, the body begins to heal itself. Medications such as mood elevators, or antidepressants can be beneficial. I am not speaking of illegal drugs which produce a temporary euphoria, but rather the prescription drugs that the medical profession creates and dispenses. These drugs stimulate the chemical responses in the human body to manufacture the chemicals that will be healing by helping to alleviate the depression that is causing destructive chemicals to be created. They allow the productive healing chemicals to begin to be created again. Initially the medication itself is bringing the better feeling, but in time, those medications will actually teach the body again how to produce the chemicals needed to feel joyous and uplifted.

Joy is one of the most healing aspects of love and it is free. Anyone is free to be joyous, to be happy and to be uplifted. It is not mandatory, it is voluntary. Some people choose to be born with the gift of joy. They are the worlds so called optimists. They are always seeing the glass half full. They always believe that no matter how bad things may be, they will become better. They are able to see goodness in all things. They are more forgiving to themselves and other people. They are able to find ways to be happy even when a situation seems almost intolerable and the reason is they believe that things will be better no matter how bad things seem to be. Thus they are able to go through crisis periods, and solve things and become joyous again more rapidly. During their difficult times their body is obviously creating chemicals that are destructive to the body, but since the depression, anxiety and unhappiness are of a much shorter duration there is not time enough for very significant bodily damage to occur. Therefore those who choose to be born with the gift of joy or develop it during their life, give themselves the potential for longer, happier and a more productive life, more feeling of self worth, more ability to bounce back from things that are frightening painful or uncomfortable. Such people may often have very difficult lives and you might rightly say, "Well if they are so happy then why do they have difficult lives?" It is because such people have the capacity to help other people learn how to be joyous. Joy is infectious. Persons who are always able to see the light at the end of the tunnel, or that things will eventually become better, may well help other people who are less joyous, through their experiences, to see that joy is a great gift. It is a healing thing. Such people may choose to become counselors, physicians or other people in the healing capacity. Through their experience and through their constant proof that everything has the potential to be a positive experience, they will not give up their belief that all things will eventually be well and be happy again. They are an inspiration to other people. They do not consciously or in a deliberate way set about to experience unhappiness in their life, but they are well equipped to handle it when it occurs. Almost all truly joyous people have two things in their consciousness: one is that they always seek to find their portion of the responsibility in anything that occurs in their life and they are unwilling to place blame fully on another person. The second is that these people are frequently able to recall the difficulty in their life that they overcame through the confident belief in the goodness of all things and teach this to others and help others through difficult times that may seem endless. You will find that the Law of Responsibility proves itself over and over again in reaction and responses of the truly joyous people to the things that occur in their lives. They will take their share of responsibility for that which is not happy and they will take, although not boastfully, their share of the responsibility for things that turn out well. They bring additional joy and benefit into their lives. Of all the emotions that humans experience, obviously love is the greatest. Love and joy are often equally involved and joy is one of the most powerful emotions that humans can experience and is one of the powerful healers in the entire universe.

UNIVERSAL SPIRITUAL LAW OF NEED

The Law of Need simply stated is that nothing in the Universe exists unless it is needed. The Law of Need is powerful creation in action, bringing to the universe a constant state of creativity for the constant needs of the universe itself in its ever growing, ever changing and ever evolving state. The Law of Need is perhaps the basic structure of the Law of Creation. Need is a powerful universal law. Indeed the universe would not exist if it were not needed.

The Law of Need is a vastly misunderstood law. It is one that is entirely important to the creation of anything. Societies' general perception of need in the area of human interaction, is that to be needy is to be weak, to be unable to fill your own life with enough substance, joy, etc. and to require at least one other human being to fulfill your needs. This is considered somewhat a weakness, and it is pointed out that self-reliant people do not need other people. This teaching is incorrect. It is true that no other human being can supply your needs. It is equally true that people do, indeed need one another. From the emotion of need comes creation. Need then is a strong creative power. If you did not need shelter, you would not create shelter. If you did not need fire, humanity would never have found fire, and the many uses that it brings. Everything begins with a need for something, or someone. If people did not need each other, children would not be born and humanity would soon cease to exist.

The very act of creation begins with a need. The very act of two humans coming together to create a new life begins with the need to be a part of someone else's life and to experience something with them. Let's briefly look at the difference between need and want. We need air to breathe, to survive in our current form, we need water, but we want nice houses, and we want to have enough money to live comfortable. Need speaks to the very things that are required for human existence. Once the basic needs are met, then comes the wanting for more things that are not needed.

The Law of Need is one of the most important attributes of creation. Without need nothing can be or will be created at the level of survival that are wanted to make survival a more pleasant thing. If there were no wants along with the needs, humans would be satisfied to have only the most basic needs met such as food, shelter and clothing. After this comes the things that add to the human experience, such as education, art and music (all the beauty of life). That which is needed is the basic survival of life. Therefore, need is a compelling creative thing. When the needs are met, the wants can then be attended to, and that which is wanted becomes a need. This increases the creative nature, increases the interaction between human beings, increase the joy that can be found in experiencing many different things in a lifetime. You do not need animal companions in your home, but once you have them you realized you do need them. They are a very important part of your life, and you an important part of theirs. Need creates the desire to need more and more of what is good and loving in one's life. It is not selfishness, it is creativity. If you did not need anything, then essentially you would cease to exist for there would be no purpose to existence. Need is a powerful drive of expression of self and interactions with other life forms. It is a basic tool of creative energy. It can be successfully argued that God needs us as much as we need God, for we are ALL aspects of God. We are all a part of the Consciousness of God. If we did not exist, what would God be? Need then is the basic driving tool of creative thinking and creative action. Need brings into existence that which is basic to life in any form. Need is that which creates cooperative action between life forms. All things that are, began because there was a need for those things to be. The more people need, the more creative they become and the more advances they make in their own well-being and in their sharing of that well-being with others.

People are drawn together in relationships because each of them needs what the other has to offer. This does not mean that they become dependent on one another in the sense that they expect another to provide everything for them that they are incapable of providing. That is a different thing entirely, it means that they openly and joyously admit that their relationship is based on the fact that person A has certain attributes, qualities, talents, areas of information that person B does not have. Person B has certain things that person A does not have, and happily they share these with one another. Each of them benefiting from the relationship. Need, then creates an ability to share. You and others or your mate are together because each of you provides things that are not a part of the personality or character of the other individual. By joining together, each of you become stronger because you are sharing with the other, your strengths. You are helping each other through your weakness. To become as one in a true bonding of the soul and each willingly and lovingly contribute their portion to the relationship, whatever the relationship might be. In a good relationship, even if it does not last forever, each person will have benefited from the relationship, will have learned things that they did not previously know, will be capable of doing things that they could not previously do, and will always remember with some fondness the relationship that they had, and the good they received and the good they shared.

Unfortunately, for many people, other elements enter in and they allow that which brought them together to decay, and they very often end up in a state where they can find no good at all that they have gained from the relationship. They are fooling themselves. If they are honest they know that in some way, every relationship between any two human beings has been mutually beneficial.

Need, then with its powerful creative aspect is a law that cannot be denied. Children need parents, parents need children, the earth needs both plant and animal life forms. This is one of the strongest needs of all, for if all animal life forms were to disappear from our planet, all plant life forms would also disappear, and if all plant life forms disappeared all animal life forms equally would disappear. Need, then is interactive, creative, and cannot be denied. To say I need nothing or no one, is never a truth, it is simply an admission that you do not know what you need. All life forms need all other life forms. There is no life form that is not needed. It is true that life forms become extinct for various reasons, but not until some other life form has developed to the point that it is able to fill the position. This is the normal order of things, but the need for every position to be filled is always there.

One of the things that has happened upon earth because the Law of Need has not been understood, is that certain life forms have been so removed from the cycle of continuity that other life forms have been allowed to multiply to a point where they are unable to exist on the amount of nourishment available to them. We at times, have an imbalance in the natural order of things upon planet earth. This has brought about concern upon the part of ecologist to restore balance that has been disturbed. Eventually that balance will be restored because it needs to be restored. If you can think of need from now on as a powerful creative force that enables you, gives you the energy to accomplish the things you wish to accomplish, acquire the things you wish to acquire, and be a more comfortable and well balanced person, then you will be able to say, "I need" without feeling that this is an admission of weakness, but rather a declaration of creative intent. For example you may say I need more financial abundance, I shall, out of this need, create financial abundance. As you say, I need my mate, my children, and my animal companion in my life, you are not being a weak individual who is unable to make it on your own, you are a strong individual able to draw to you persons, and other life forms that will increase your ability to love, and increase the number of life forms that you can share love with. It increases your ability to accept love from many different life forms. When you say I need my job or profession, this is not a weakness. It is a declaration of a person who knows that he or she is good at what they do and is a needed part of the human life experience.

The more you are able to say, I need, the more you are claiming your own creative abilities. Those who cannot admit to needing, are stifling the very essence of creativity itself. For those, however who expect others to do for them, and who are seeking in another, the thing that they do not have in their self, with expectation that others will provide for them, all that they do not have are not using need in a creative way. This is a parasitic use of the Law of Need. They are trying to take from another, what they do not have, when in fact in true need it is a sharing of what I have with what you have, and in turn what you have with what I have. This is the proper use of need. For example to admit that your mate is a more outwardly loving person than you, is not to say that you expect him or her to take care of that entire area of human existence between the two of you, because you cannot do it. It is to say that there is something they are better at than you and you are learning to be better at it. Your mate might in turn, see in you a more practical nature in the area of finances, and rather than expecting you to always bear the burden of the financial need of the family, they could make the decision to learn more about these things themselves, be wiser in spending habits, and thus become a more functioning partner. When two persons do this, their needs are being met, but they are being met in a creative not parasitic fashion. So you see that need takes on a different unique valuable meaning in the universal sense. So understand the creative value and meaning of need and put it to work for you to achieve your wants and goals in conjunction with the other universal laws relating to creation.

Universal Spiritual Law of Need and Healing

All of life has needs. The greatest need of all life is to learn to love unconditionally. Every life form should naturally chooses its own needs in order to meet this goal. So need and love are closely related. People need one another. There are few humans or other life forms upon our planet that do not need humans or others of different life forms. An example of need and healing capacity exists between the interaction of animal life forms and plant life forms upon our planet. Humans exhale gases necessary for plant life forms. The plant life form needs the animal to be healthy and they need animal life forms in proximity to them. Plant life forms exude gases needed by animal life. Animals need plants to be healthy. Should all the plant life upon our planet die simultaneously, soon thereafter the animal life would die. This is a stunning example of the Law of Need as it interacts with healing. Demonstrating that need is a healing and even a life saving attribute of all life forms. Because of the need of animals and plant life forms, need created a way for animals and plants life forms to interact with one another. Need is an extremely creative healing form. Think of this, a young mother is faced with an experience that may result in her death. The experience happens and she is given a choice to come to the spirit world or stay on the earth plane with her children. Her children need her. This creates healing energy that causes her to say, "I shall continue in a physical life form because I'm needed, my energy is needed by my children," so the healing occurs. This happens thousands of times each day, a young mother is ill and could pass to the spirit world (die) or has been in an accident. Her children's need brings about the energy to begin the healing process. It is often called a miracle by medical science but it is need acting as the healing energy bringing about changes in the physical body.

Humans need to eat if they are to remain healthy and thus humans do what is necessary to keep their physical body healthy and to meet their physical needs. If the human race wishes to continue upon planet earth there is a need for human males and females to interact in ways that will produce a child. Love drives them together, the need to procreate is a very healing thing, for it ensures a continuation of the human race. Need provides incentive. People work for a living because they know that if they do not provide for themselves they may shorten their life span. Thus need creates the desire to learn how to do a certain profession, and obtain the necessary income to provide sustenance for themselves and family members.

Need is highly creative in healing ways. Need will bring about healing in what seems to be unhealable conditions. The need on the part of a person to be healthy and well, when fully in its creating mode, changes the physical structure of the body. Healing begins immediately and continues until the need is met. If humans and other life forms had no needs they would cease to exist in a physical way and would exist only in spiritual ways. Make no mistake, the need to be healthy creates the chemicals for health initiated by the thought and belief process. The need to live, creates procreation and the need to love brings life forms together to share. When two persons each need one another, that brings about a situation which has the potential to make both of them healthier. This does not mean a relationship in which the two persons both feel needy and unable or unwilling to do for themselves, what someone else will do for them. This is not creative need, this is destructive need. But when two mature intelligent beings willingly and lovingly enter into a relationship with one another and both of them are aware that they have needs and both of them are aware that the other person also has needs and both are willing to share their intelligence, strength and capabilities with the other they have a stable relationship, for it is equal. Perhaps one person is shy the other outgoing, but each of them recognizes that their interaction with one another can help them to enjoy life more. When need is met, the relationship becomes stable and loving and sharing. In this way need is healing.

When one person wishes to have all of their needs met but has nothing to give in return because they sought only a partner who would fulfill their needs they have a relationship that is unhealthy. Need makes people work at creating what they require to become healthy and to stay healthy. Need and joy are closely aligned, for a joyous person recognizes their own needs and seeks to meet them, but not through vandalizing another. A joyous person recognizes that they must bring to any relationship all that they can.

You can imagine how well two basically joyous persons, both of them mature enough to recognized need and to engage in the creative processes of fulfilling needs will joyously share with one another. A friendship of such dimension and a love of such dimension will be successful and healthy.

Comments/Examples Law of Need

Being healthy/healed begins with the desire and need to be healthy. Creating or manifesting the healing then carried out through the application of the Universal Spiritual Laws as I will illustrate. Unfortunately many people apply the Law of Karma in a negative way. They believe because they have been taught for generations, that they need to be punished for something negative they chose to do (Law of Freedom of Choice) in the past. However by understanding and applying Universal Spiritual Laws in a positive way they could take responsibility (Law of Responsibility) for what they did and choose to forgive themselves and others involved (Law of Forgiveness). Then by the Law of Love, they can love themselves and the others and create a positive and healing attitude filled with joy (Law of Joy) and harmony (Law of Harmony). This would help balance (Law of Balance) their past negative karma, bringing spiritual progression and healing. Only the truth (Law of Truth) and understanding of Universal Spiritual Laws allows you to fulfill your need (Law of Need) of being healed. So you see how all the laws work together when followed in a positive way to elevate your physical and spiritual life, starting with the desire and need to do so.

So you see that the Law of Need is a vastly misunderstood law and it is one that is entirely important to the creation of anything. So the discussion of the Law of Need should change your whole perception of need as being a somewhat weakness vs a true strength and source of creation. It's truly sad how mankind has taken so many concepts or life's guidelines/important laws and changed them either due to a lack of proper understanding or to benefit themselves. This is a truly important principle and truth to be aware of when you are dealing with any historical book whether it is the Bible or any other book concerning historical events or speech. Remember neither God nor Jesus wrote the bible. Rulers in power decided its content. For example the first Ecumenical Council was convened by Roman Emperor Constantine I in 325 AD. The books of the bible were chosen by the Bishop and Constantine I and changes were made by following ecumenical councils.

15

UNIVERSAL SPIRITUAL LAW OF CHANGE

The Law of Change is a dynamic law indeed. It is quite evident that all that we have already spoken of indicates that change is a universal and observable law. Without change, all life would cease to exist. This is impossible, of course. Change is the law that keeps all of the action moving in a constantly creative direction. Change is not random, change is a careful law, all change is change for the better. The Law of Change directs everything that happens in the created universe. Change is a very important law because it is the one constant in the universe. It is thus an aspect of love that is essentially governed by love in the most profound and direct sense. The Universal Mind, frequently called God, is love in action. Nothing can grow, evolve, expand, contract or do anything else at all without change. The very universe, physical and spiritual, would cease to exist if change were not a law of God.

Another way to state the Law of Change is that change is the essence of any life and the essence of any possibility. Consider the possibility, without change, possibility does not exist. Let us take human physical life. A human physical life begins life at a moment when change occurs. The male provides the sperm, the female provides the egg. Both egg and sperm are possibilities. Change ignites them into further possibility, then thousands, millions, billions of changes occur to produce a healthy human baby. Changes occur in the fetus and the female parent. Change occurs in the mind and emotions of everyone around the fetus. The grandparent, aunts, uncles, friends, coworkers, all undergo change as a result of this happening. Change is possibility, all things are possible because change is a continuing thing.

If it were a static situation, then, the sperm would remain within the male, the egg within the female and nothing would happen, no possibility. Change is the possibility of anything at all. The entire universe is change when the conception of one human being occurs, it is ignited with endless possibility. Thus, the Law of Change is every possibility coexisting eternally. Without change, nothing is possible. Change must continue to be, or nothing will exist. Persons who desire no changes will, of course, not be able to achieve this. It is a manifest impossibility. They will make every effort, however in the areas they think they can control to not permit change. Those who embrace the law of loving change and all change that is based upon love, lead lives that are ever exciting, ever looking forward to the next change in their life. The change could be as tiny as a decision between a married couple who have been neglecting the affection side of their relationship, to begin each day with a warm and loving kiss and embrace, and wishing to one another a good and happy and prosperous day. It can be as immense as changing the boundaries between two nations through an act of war or peaceful decision to do so. Change is to be enthusiastically accepted as the most important part of existence. One, then must carefully think about the changes they wish to make in their life. You are going to change, but you have the option of deciding what those changes will be, rather than simply allowing them to happen. Those who enthusiastically begin each day aware that there will be changes in their lives will plan for the changes that they want to occur. They will plan them out and take steps to enable them to achieve the desired changes. They will approach each opportunity with great enthusiasm. They will help others in decision making. They will talk constantly and think constantly in the subconscious and frequently conscious areas of their minds, of what changes are necessary to facilitate their desires. Remember, desire is also a child of change and a necessary child of change. They will enthusiastically work toward their desired goals.

Since you cannot avoid change, embrace it, love it, live with it and do all that you can to make those changes the ones of a positive and beneficial nature for yourself and others. This is love in action. Patients come to physicians for a change in their life and health. Healing is change, it changes conditions, emotions and mentality. It changes things about the person who is undergoing healing, the person who is providing the healing energy and everyone surrounding both healer and patient. This is why healing is love in action, for it is eternal change.

For many reasons change is often feared by people. Someone's reasons are fear, laziness, familiarity and lack of adventure. Since change is inevitable and cannot be avoided in the long run, one should learn to expect it, work with it, bend with it and welcome it. Obviously we should all strive for positive and constructive change that will benefit everyone. As the saying goes, "If you can't bend with change, you may well break". Change can be exciting and certainly not boring. Therefore it can add a lot to your life.

Ronald L. Cole, M.D.

Universal Spiritual Law of Change and Healing

The Law of Change is an interesting law, in that it is one that people attempt to dismiss or break, but of course, it is not possible to do so. For change is the only constant of the universe. Each thought, word and deed causes change. The change is positive when the thought, word or deed or combination thereof is positive. When the changes are negative, the chemicals in the body are producing negative activity, which if left alone long enough, will produce physical symptoms within or upon the physical body. Change is a part of healing because everything that happens is change. There is no thing, no word, or thought that is not change, something changes. This is true not only of your physical body but is true with your interaction with other human beings. Each moment which you spend with another being, produces change in both of you. When you speak before groups of people, you are changing and everyone in the group is changing. The entire mental, emotional, spiritual and physical self is undergoing constant change.

In healing then, this means that you have control over the changes that are happening to your mind, emotions, soul, spirit, body and affairs. There is nothing that is not constantly changing and you have the right to control the change. You cannot stop change from happening, but you can control what is changing and how it is changing. Thus the changes in your physical being are dependent on your thoughts, words, and deeds. If you are ill in any way, in discomfort, your thought pattern will keep you ill or begin the process of bringing healing about. Therefore it would be wise for all humans to include in their thought process several times daily this simple prayer/affirmation I gave you earlier, "I am changing with every thought, word and deed. I choose positive change, I choose health and I choose to think, speak, and act in loving ways for my health to remain in its most perfect state." Change is vital to healing, change creates that which is either healing energy or destructive energy.

You can easily prove this with two persons, one vital, upbeat, creative, loving and energetic who will enjoy good health. They may have the occasional discomfort or pain, but they will not allow themselves to become a part of this to make the pain the center of their life. They will actively engage in whatever is necessary to bring about health again. The opposite is the pessimist, the one who sees everything as bad, hopeless, and who is usually in some kind of mental, emotional or physical difficulty most of the time. They cannot understand why the changes their body is undergoing are painful. They see no brightness, they cannot see a positive way and they perceive that the glass is half-empty. When they change that thought process, and some do, they begin to become healthy again. Change is always going on. You are responsible for what the change will be. The optimists are healthy individuals and possibly a few physical discomforts, but they work activity and have the undying belief that they shall be completely healed. This is the difference between themselves and others who constantly bring pain, grief and disaster into their life and who do not know how to see the glass as half-full. They create one crisis after another in their life because they operate out of fear and fear is a most debilitating thing. The changes within them continue to be negative while the changes in the optimist continue to be positive. If you have a pessimist in your family or friends you can actively pray that they will learn to love themselves, care for themselves and let the changes be of a positive nature. So change is inevitable and you have a great deal of control over your changes, including your health status. Make the changes in your life positive and loving ones so you can enjoy what they bring into your life including good health and healing.

UNIVERSAL SPIRITUAL LAW OF ESSENCE

16

The Law of Essence states that all things have a central point of being, called essence. The Law of Essence holds all things, all beings, all creation into itself with self-awareness, the essence of all things is of course generally put, what is called God. It is more, even than that. It is self-awareness. Essence, then is what holds each aspect of creation into its individualized expression of self. Essence is the very concentrated self-awareness, and of course it is God. The Law of Essence is the law of that which in its purest form, it is the beginning of a thing, a concept, an idea, a goal, an essential part of everything. Essence is primarily creativity available for use in any form at all. Essence is love, and love is essence. Love is the very essence of everything in existence and love is in everything that exists. The Law of Essence, then in correlation to love, aids in the changing of pure love into spiritual and physical form, durability, action, and these are the things that are needful for something to be successful, for something to be desirable. A very simple example is that which happens when physical flowers are reduced to what perfumers call essential oils. From the physical flower is extracted the very essence which provides scent to the flower. Now, you have physical evidence of the Law of Essence. The desire is to gain that which gives the flower its scent and through change use it in other ways, which is extremely spiritual. The flower growing in its native place, whether it be a well-tended garden, a meadow or a woodland, will share its essence with essentially a limited few life forms, including humans who are physically close to the place where the flower is. When the flower has been taken down to the essence of its fragrance, the fragrance may be distributed to many thousands of people who otherwise would not have had the opportunity to enjoy the scent of the flower.

Thus, flowers happily share their essence. They do not object to being lovingly plucked and give up their life spirit, if their scent energy or essence remains that it might be shared by many. There are those who believe that to pluck flowers may be a cruel act, it is not, if the flowers are plucked in love and if those who are plucking the flowers are planning to use them that many may enjoy their essence. The essence, once extracted may be used to create many wonderful things through the Law of Essence with its eternal melding with the Law of Change. Of course it has been long discovered that scent is one of the most potent senses for stimulating emotions, memory, etc. Thus, essence is also, in a very real sense, when it is applied to certain human sensitivities a tool to create greater enjoyment of life.

In the metaphysical use of essence, the metaphysician will seek the core of truth. They will read, study, meditate, to find the essence of what is. Without this desire for essence and without the Law of Essence, again, nothing could be accomplished. Every thought has its essence, every word, every deed, has an essence. This, of course, can be a two way thing, for while every word has its essence or its core meaning, not all human consciousness responds to every word in the same way. Different cultures use different words to describe the same thing. Therefore language often fails in communication. The essence of the word does not change, but the interpretation may.

Let us use the word love, most people would generally agree that love should be nurtured, cared for, responded to, shared, given, received, in a harmonious and helpful way. Let us consider some of the things that are done in the name of love. Wars have been fought, families have been abandoned, cultural clashes occur between people who love different things, and cannot agree on which is right, so they perform acts of violence. The essence of love remains, the action of persons are what change, not the essence. Essence is a harder thing to explain than some of the other laws because in itself, by its very meaning, it is what makes universal law work. The essence of universal law is love, the primary law. Universally, the primary law is always in action, but life forms throughout the universe frequently act in ways that are not within the Law of Love. First of all, they do not understand the Law of Love. When the Law of Love is understood, all laws are followed automatically.

The Law of Essence is that which enables all universal law to act in harmony with one another, within the primary Law of Love. A concept you may have to meditate upon. Essence is the most basic component of everything and that is why it is the basic component of Universal Law.

When we look at putting the Law of Essence to work, we find that it is already at work. It is often good to seek the essence of all that you do. For instance, let us look at the example of when persons become irritated with one another. They speak without thinking, thus they are not seeking the essence of the irritation itself, but rather are adding to it. If persons on the edge of an irritated interaction would separate themselves from one another for a period of time, and speak the true source of their irritation, which might have nothing to do with the current disagreement, they might then be able to quietly seek answers together, to solve, heal and change the true irritant, rather than the harshness and accusatory activities of fighting.

Things are rarely what they seem to be through human

consciousness. Humans who work to find the essence in what is happening in their life are bound to have better and more harmonious lives. It is a practical thing, it is a searching for truth and this is always beneficial. Persons have a tendency not to go as deeply into their emotions, thoughts and actions as would be beneficial, and actually it is because they fear to find what is there. Honest effort to seek the essence of one's thought patterns will result in great self-revelation and assist in making the changes necessary to a more harmonious life pattern.

Universal Spiritual Law of Essence and Healing

The Law of Essence is a fascinating one. While directly involved in healing it is not as easy to explain as some of the prior laws. Essence is that which is the very basic part or core of what something or someone is. In a human being, the essence of the human is their souls or spirit, that which is eternal. It is also the essence of any other life form. Essence also is the chemical structure of any life form. It is the thing that is most closely associated with the life form. Because it is the most closely associated, all essence naturally has healing energy that can be used for healing. Let's take flowers for example. The physical essence of a flower is the portion of its chemical makeup which results in the scent of the floral arrangement. This can be extracted from the flower in its purest chemical form and be used as an essential oil, a healing property to be placed upon a physical body as aroma therapy and in many other ways. Checking the contents of many of the things that humans eat and place upon their body, you will see evidence of the essence of plant life. The reason that essence heals is very simple. It is because all life forms upon our planet, be it animal, plant or mineral are in perfect harmony with all other life forms.

Certain life forms do not have all of the same chemicals and other life forms do have all of the same chemicals. But whatever the chemical essence of a life form, all life forms are in harmony because the essence of life is the same, the soul and spirit. The physical essence of life is the same, therefore it is not actually true that one life form can be allergic to another life form. It will be hard for most people to understand or accept this concept. Humans believe themselves allergic to certain plants or animals, or foods because they have created this untrue belief. These types of beliefs and realities, mankind has created over many thousands of years and we now unnecessarily have made our daily life governed by them. It certainly would not be easy to eliminate them from our culture since we have locked them into our belief system but maybe if we start now we can slowly eliminate the belief. Chemicals that are necessary to every life form upon the planet would not be disastrous to one another or life would cease to exist. Thus in using essence in healing, we must work not only with the essence of the life forms, such as aroma therapy but also converting plants into medicines that humans can take for healing purposes. Plant life forms do not object to humans using their essence for healing purposes. The interaction of plant life and animal life is a necessary part of life upon the planet. If it did not exist the essence of the gases of plant life and human life could not interact and there could be no plant life or human life.

Those who find themselves allergic to other life forms are following a created myth that has no true reality, scientifically speaking, and I'm not speaking of science as humans perceive it but, true science, universal science, Universal Law. It would be difficult to get an allergist to accept this universal truth. I think you can get insight to this universal truth by the fact that not ALL humans are allergic to poison ivy, peanuts or many other plants or substances. The Law of Love, the dominant law, says there can be no conflict between life forms. They are naturally suitable to one another. They naturally have a symbiotic relationship to one another. It is the essence of whatever is, that has the symbiotic relationship to everything else. Therefore essence is a law that is necessary in the art of healing for if that law did not exist there could be no coming together of that which is the bases of every life form to interact favorably with every other life form. The Law of Essence says simply, the essential soul, spirit and physical expression of every life form is symbiotic with every other life form and is therefore a portion of the healing energy of every life form. This is Universal Law. Without essence there is no healing. With essence fully understood or even partially understood and accepted as truth, humans would cease to believe that their body cannot comfortably accommodate the essences of another life forms.

UNIVERSAL SPIRITUAL LAW OF TRUTH

The Law of Truth is that there is only truth. Truth is a portion of the substance that holds all of the universe together. It is the law that holds chaos at bay. The underlying truth of the universe is the "Cosmic Equation" God is One, One is All, All is God. This truth, the foundation of all creation, is the very Law of Truth. Truth is law, and law is truth. Without truth in its universal sense, absolute chaos would be the rule, this cannot happen, it is impossible. Truth is one of the strongest universal laws, and whether it seems it is being obeyed or not is irrelevant. It is being obeyed.

Truth always has been, always will be, truth is unchanging in its being, but it always is being added to. Truth is a growing and evolving thing, but that which is basically true remains truth. Thus, it is basically true that love is the primary law of the universe, but love is a changing, growing thing. This can be demonstrated simply by the evolvement of love in human actions. It is a changing thing, but truth remains truth. God is Love, is an unchanging truth, but understanding of that unchanging truth is in itself a changing truth.

It was previously stated that the Law of Change is at work in everything. It was also stated that the Universal Laws are immutable, which means they cannot change. These might seem to be contradictory expressions. They are not contradictory, everything changes. God's Law is immutable. What brings them together is that God's Law is immutable in its concept, but in order to be active, to work, it must evolve. How, then does truth evolve? It evolves through a simple thing to say, but often not acted upon, understanding. The basic chord of truth cannot change they are immutable. Because change is absolutely necessary, concepts and understandings change, possibilities change, that which was not doable at one stage in universal evolution becomes a doable thing. The truth has not changed, the ability to understand and use the truth has changed. So in that sense one could say truth has changed. These are mystical things that do not lend themselves well to human words We are not yet physically, mentally, emotionally or spiritually evolved to the point that we could fully understand this. The Law of Truth removes all limitations. Truth is without limits. It is an expanding, growing, evolving thing which simultaneously remains exactly what it is, truth. So we see that there is a great difference between universal truth and human truth. As stated there is but one universal truth and that is God or Creation and the laws that govern it. On the other hand man's truths are often a product of interpretation, manipulation, prejudice and ignorance. Man's truth varies from person to person, group to group, country to country and religion to religion. As an example, there are hundreds of "one true religions" in the world. So what does that tell a logical thinking intelligent person? Universal Laws and Truths rise above all religions and countries. There is a statement in the Bible, and it is a statement that is found in all great works that seek to uplift mankind, "Ye shall know the truth, and the truth shall make you free". This is in itself a very basic truth, but humans do not always know the truth. They know only their truth, and they too often attempt to make their truth the truth of others through any means available.

True higher spiritual enlightenment is a knowing of the truth at the level the receiver is prepared to understand. Remember there are many levels of understanding and consciousness. So as each individual evolves spiritually their understanding of truth moves to a higher level also. In fact that is what evolution is all about, a growing in the understandings and applications of universal truths.

So beware of the many bearing the truth and if their truths are not based on the principle of love than it is not of highest level of truth. Look deep within yourself and ask for the truth and allow it to come to you. This is what is stated above as knowing the truth. True knowing comes from the God Consciousness that is a part of all of us. When one knows something received from the God Consciousness, it is inevitably truth, and almost always has a marked effect upon the life pattern of the individual who now knows the truth. In most instances, for that individual there is a beneficial thing, for truth itself is healing. For others, it may be too frightening for them to accept, for it then demands responsibility, and for many, responsibility is a hard thing to accept.

The Age of Aquarius or the age of responsibility is upon us and with that added knowing of self responsibility,the consciousness of humanity will continue its evolvement at a more accelerated rate and truth will be an easier understanding.

Universal Spiritual Law of Truth and Healing

All human beings have heard the word truth, but do not understand it. Truth is truth, never changing and truth claims itself in the metaphysical aspects of every pattern that humans have ever had. The knowing that human life and all life is a part of God. Truth says God is One, One is All, All is God. This is the basic truth of the universe but to humans perception of truth can be anything at all. Truth is essential to healing, for "Ye shall know the truth and the truth shall set you free". Truth is one of the catalyst of healing. When a human being sees the truth of an ailment whether it be minor or major and that truth is that they must change their thought pattern, using the Law of Change, into personal responsibility and loving themselves, and seeing themselves worthy of using the Law of Truth. Then begins the process of healing. It is an untruth that humans must suffer. It is a manmade lie, that it is the fate of humans to suffer, because of original sin. There has been no such thing, there cannot be such a thing. Truth is truth, but for complete and permanent healing truth must be the catalyst. There is not pain, nor original sin, no reason for suffering. When truth is accepted, healings may be miraculously swift, but as long as the truth is neglected, it can be difficult for healing to occur. The Law of Truth is not only necessary, but catalytic to maintaining good health. I have seen this in my practice, when I help someone to understand that they do not need to be ill and that help is available and they may choose to accept it and responsibly use it. I find that they become well much more quickly. I, of course, must use my inner instincts to know which patients can accept and understand it and put it to use. This is the Law of Truth in action. Truth is hard to understand, for it has been so sadly abused and neglected by human perception. But the greatest truth that exist, is the truth that GOD IS IN EVERYTHING. The Essence of God in all that is and is that essence, soul, spirit and divinity that says it is natural to be healthy. It is not natural to be less than healthy. When this truth ignites the consciousness of any life form, freedom happens, health happens, truth happens, truth is a great healer. This is the truth.

18

UNIVERSAL SPIRITUAL LAW OF PURITY

The Law of Purity, simply stated means that essentially everything that exists is pure, within itself it is pure. The purity stems from the simple fact that everything that exists is God, and God could not be other than pure. The Law of Purity, then is the law that states God is all, and all is God. That is the purity that controls and created the entire universe. All things in the essence are absolutely pure, for they are absolute God. Purity, in the universal sense has nothing to do with manmade laws, ideology, interest and acceptance. It is simply that all is God and that is absolute purity in itself. God expresses self in infinite forms, substance, etc. Manmade laws defining what persons may do and not do come from the intuitive understanding that the essence of all is God.

Purity and essence are love. The universe is completely itself, God is completely itself, which is everything that is. God in essence is unadulterated and pure. The universe, equally so. The Universal Law of Purity, maintains that whatever may seem to be the case to individualized perception, the universe is absolutely pure. The universe continues to be all that is created and will continue to create.

In the efforts to maintain purity however, mankind of course makes laws that are unenforceable, but still the essence of that Pure God Self is never far from the consciousness of all living things, whether they are physically living or spiritually living. When you honestly know these simple facts of universal truth and law, much of the confusion that surrounds acting, being and believing becomes clearer and you will simply see the purity, the God in all that is. There is nothing else, therefore there is nothing but purity. All things that seem to be impure are merely in the consciousness of the beholder. Anything that seems not to be God is in the consciousness of the beholder. In reality, there cannot be anything that is impure, for there cannot be anything that is not God. That is a simple explanation which when truly understood relieves all life forms of any attempt to interfere in one another's process of expressing their own pure Godhood. Mankind, in their human essence cannot create anything that is absolutely pure. Mankind, in their true Godself, was begun with absolute purity. Therefore there is essentially no reason to attempt to crate purity, it already is.

Humans, for instance, have over the centuries in many cultures, and groups of people insisted on sexual purity for their females of marriageable age. A high premium has been administered for a sexually pure female, and virginity a prized thing. The essence of a female is not her sexual self, it's her Godself. Humans were seeking purity in an area that has absolutely nothing to do with true divine purity, but it is to the credit of the human race, that they at least attempt purity. It is not to the credit of the human race that they demanded it of their females and in many cultures, punished females who are less than pure while not demanding the same purity of the male portion of the group society.

When something is intrinsically pure, it needs no human laws to create purity. Therefore, many laws that humans have made to create purity have been made because instinctively, and intuitively humans did not understand that they are pure, they are God and that nothing more needed to be done to insure purity than to accept your Godhood, and work within the areas of spiritual self, rather than concentrating upon the physical being of self. Physically no one can be pure Purity means uncontaminated, unadulterated, single substance. There are thousands of substances in your human self, and not even the substances themselves are pure, for they interact with one another in order that your physical being might continue. Your essence, your total self, is already pure, it requires no tinkering, no laws, no help, nothing but to be accepted, honored and worked with.

When the above principles of purity and God are discerned, many people will question the statement that if all is God then what about all the thoughts, words and deeds that occur in the world that are considered bad or evil. Does this mean that a part of God is bad or evil? Remember when we use terms bad and evil, we are using man-made terms and concepts. These terms in many ways are relative terms. In other words, what is defined as wrong, bad or evil to one person, group or society may be looked at as acceptable in another. This does not mean it is the best for all of society, that every person or group should make up their own acceptable code of behavior, but it does point out the very man-made concept of what is right and wrong. We have had groups, institutions and governments that have been more than anxious to establish those exacting definitions for us to adhere to. One should look close at times to discover whose purpose is really being served by hard and fast rules, the rule makers or those who are to be governed by them? The concept of good and evil is more of a man-made concept that is often used to manipulate people. When people simple follow God's laws of love there is no such thing as evil. The concept of evil may well be a concept of learning, and growing as one evolves to this level of living God's Universal Laws of Love.

In most societies mankind has already found what satisfies them.

They have divided God into two parts, the loving God and the devil God- the fallen angel. They have even assigned to the so-called evil forces, equal power with God, and equal creative ability. It is not quite that easy, it does not happen in that way, it is a comfortable myth that is only a myth. No one really understands what evil is. No one really knows what is good, and what is bad. Societies make their own judgements on what is wrong. From a more universal point of view, unmitigated evil, somewhat loses its definition and it is difficult to find terms to explain what is evil and what is not. These things are purely human conception, they have little to do with reality at the Universal level.

Humans consider violence to be an evil thing, and certainly it is to their credit that they wish to reduce violence upon our planet, but violence exists elsewhere. It is actually part of Universal acceptability, for planets are born and die. Suns are born and die, black holes are created. It is difficult to put the truth of this concept into acceptable words since so many previous beliefs are based on guilt, fear and good and evil. One way to possibly try to provide insight to this concept is to point out that much of what humans think of as evil is only evolution. All things happen for a purpose, a learning experience to aid evolution and raise our consciousness. Of course, humans should treat each other with love and consideration, should perform no acts of violence against one another, not verbal, mental, emotional or physical, but what is called evil in these acts, from the Universal level is a learning experience. It is part of understanding who and what you are.

Even though humans are pure, they do the things they do because most people have not been taught or realize that they are a part of God, do not believe that they are pure, and even more importantly, do not believe that anyone is pure, and that it is perhaps their right to try and force their ideas of purity upon others. When all humans on planet earth know who they are, these things, we call evil will cease to exist. Those persons who have already accepted that they are a part of God do not do acts of violence. It is not part of their ability. This sounds simplistic because it is. So as one learns through life's lessons and experiences, they evolve spiritually which raises the level of their thoughts, words and deeds from a less than loving level to a loving level.

Remember the other Universal Laws of Cause and Effect, Karma and others which teach that you reap what you sow. So your less loving acts will present you with less pleasant lessons that you must learn or repeat until you do. Due to centuries of different teachings and beliefs, one must give this concept of right and wrong a great deal of thought and not use what is being said here as an excuse to act in a less than loving ways.

Another way to look at this dilemma of social behavior is to realize that we have not been taught what our real essence truly is and that is a spiritual part of the God creation. Thus we are rather immature in our understandings of self, so our behavior is also rather unrefined and less loving or positive. We do the best we can but with increased understanding and growth, our behavior will also improve to a more evolved and positive level and the negative actions and occurrences in our society will decrease.

It's just like teaching young children proper behavior and seeing them grow into more loving people and taking responsibility for themselves and their behavior. That is probably the essence of self-responsibility, governing one's self in ways that are conducive to a better life for one's self and an interactive life for all life forms with whom we share our planet. As long as humans are willing to be violent to any life form, there will be evil. Within the human consciousness, not within our pure God consciousness, it is often difficult to recognize and accept that there is equality within all life forms. For the purity of God includes all creation. We usually see ourselves as a superior life form, and it is the belief that it is alright to eliminate life forms of what is considered a lesser level. Only when humans have chosen, non-violent activity will the essential purity, that is life itself, manifest itself in every way. So it might be simple to say, examine yourself and ask if you are capable of committing an act of deliberate violence against any life form at all. Would you deliberately kill an insect in your home, cut down a tree because it interferes with your flower garden, shoot a bird because it had made a nest where you did not want a nest to be or kill another human being because that human being was interfering in your lifestyle by being where you did not wish them to be. All of these things are exactly the same. They are aberrations of purity. Genocide, as committed by certain human beings to purify the race, make certain that those of conceived lesser value do not continue to exist, for they pollute the race. That, of course is a travesty, and completely wrong. In the consciousness of the person who commits genocide, they are doing an act of purity, when in fact they are desecrating their very humanity by going against the Law of Purity, which says all is pure, all is God, leave it alone to express its Godhood. Do not attempt to exterminate it. Many will find this law difficult, indeed to understand, it is an interesting law, and it is a powerful law, it is not an easily understood law. So the true outward expression of purity comes with understanding our true essence. One can look at the Law of Purity, that it is simply, a knowingness of what you are, your true essence. Some people feel that mankind is basically evil, others say mankind is basically pure. This law simply presents a knowingness of our true and basic essence of what we are, that indeed we are a part of

God. There is a tremendous amount of criticism voiced against this truth as one would expect. That does not change the fact that it is true. Many important truths have been denied by mankind for as long as it can be hidden. The sooner we learn the true rules of life the sooner we can start living life to its intended fullness. Remember the true essence of God is pure unconditional love so if one wishes to think of themselves as God, let them express this love and the world would and will be a much better place for all of God's creations.

The simple truth remains, nothing in the universe is basically evil, all is God. That being said however, there are individuals, groups or organizations in both the physical and spiritual realms that, because of their negative beliefs and lack of higher understandings, do not act in loving ways which could be considered unacceptable or evil. The simple truth remains upon earth, the chief reason that persons do not accept their Godhood is that they have been taught not to accept it and that God is apart from humanity. Over many centuries mankind has come to accept certain authority figures or groups as "keepers of the truth" and believe what they say without question. Blind faith and belief often does not uncover the real truth but often meets the needs or desires of those teaching the "claimed truth". It is felt by some that people would use this knowledge to idolize themselves. Those that may choose to do this, would only do so because they do not truly understand what God is. God is not violent, God is not arbitrary, God is not determined to bend all other life forms to the will of God. These are not God qualities. It all comes down to, when we talk of purity to whether or not individual parts of God have the spiritual maturity to understand what God is, and to understand that God is still in the process of being God, and ever will be. God is not static, God is an ever evolving consciousness. How could it be otherwise?

Whatever is taught of God, is what can be taught of the evolution of God in the now, but the evolution of God is the evolution of consciousness and is an eternal thing. For unless God were evolving, there would be no God, and essentially there would be nothing. All things must evolve, change, learn, grow and be. You are God, evolving, changing, learning. Therefore, this law will be one of the most difficult for many to truly accept. They must go against generations of teaching to the contrary. Will people ever accept it? Yes,of course they will, but perhaps not for a very long time. It is a law that requires basic conscious changes in the very essence of human belief.

Let's use this very simple analogy. If a child places their hand on a hot stove, it is bad, but the child is unlikely to do it a second time, having experienced the pain. They will avoid the stove in the future, and eventually as they mature will be taught by their parents how to use it safely, and in ways that will not cause them pain and anguish. In the evolution, then of humans in their expression of their Godhood, they may touch the stove, and learn that this is not a good idea. They may do others things with equally undesirable results. They may, instead play with matches or a lighter, and burn themselves, and then discover that these are not things to be played with, but useful tools.

All of these things, then are simply evidence of infancy in your own understanding and expression of Godhood, and as you mature, you begin to choose not to act in ways that will cause grief and unhappiness to other persons. You also, and usually this comes later, choose not to act in ways that will bring grief into your own life. That, in itself is evident of the fact, that basically, even to human consciousness, the purity of God is stronger than the consciousness of man that allows them to experiment, and must allow them to experiment. It is common that most people more quickly cease to be abusive to others than they cease to be abusive to themselves.

Being absolutely responsible for ones thoughts, words and deeds, also means that you treat yourself with love, respect and admiration. So we obviously have a lot to learn from the Law of Purity but it does provide us with very important insights and truths. Give it a little time to sink in and think about it with a very open, objective and loving mind.

Ronald L. Cole, M.D.

Universal Spiritual Law of Purity and Healing

The law of purity covers many different ideas and ideology. Purity, just in its own essence of what the word means, the purest essence of the thing that is, is a healing energy. Pure truth is a healing energy. Purity of the body through proper cleansing, eating, exercise and resting naturally contributes to the health of the individual. Different groups of people perceive purity differently. Some groups believe in ritual hand washing, other believe in total immersion baptism as a purifying trait, thus mankind intuitively recognizes the healing power of purity. Pure thoughts are thoughts that are loving. We are told to think pure thoughts by many religions and they are right. When thoughts are pure they are naturally healing to the body of the person who is thinking the thoughts. The Law of Purity simply stated, is that everything is innately pure, for it is a part God and God is pure love, pure loving creative energy, infinite energy and eternal energy. It is the perception of humans that something is impure. Nothing is. Just knowing this can create physical health. As you recall we previously discussed the manmade creation or condition called allergies and it has been engrained, like countless other conditions and beliefs, into human lives. For thousands of years humans have believed that certain things cause certain undesirable results. They pass the belief and information on to their children while the children are very young and can't really reason for themselves. They are not to eat such and such, or touch such and such, or breath such and such for it will make them sick or kill them. Obviously, with thousands of years of mankind's creative energy establishing many beliefs which have become what we perceive as the truth so therefore it happens. Would it be possible, say through understanding, accepting and applying the Law of Purity, to eliminate many ailments? In order to do that, there would have to be a significant change in the very long established beliefs. We as physicians would not simply stop treating significant ailments and tell the patient they will be fine.

So, you can see how we got off the God given "path" long ago and it will be very difficult to return to the "perfect garden of Eden". This certainly does not mean we should, "throw up our hands" and say that would be impossible, so let's just live with our created belief systems. That is just the opposite reason I am writing and publishing this book and I would hope you will put the TRUTH to work so your life will greatly improve. Obviously this would be a true challenge.

Jesus spoke truth when he said, "It is not what you put into your body through your mouth, but what comes out of your mind through your mouth which causes disease". Thoughts, words and beliefs cause disease. God does not cause disease!

The Law of Purity states simply and clearly: All that God creates is in and of itself pure. It can only be adulterated by human thinking. Humans assign impurities to other humans and to other life forms. When there are religious wars, it is because "My religion is purer than yours so you do not deserve to live because you are not pure". When it is an ethnic war, it is because, "My ethnic ancestry and my own self are purer than you, therefore you do not deserve to live". Purity is much abused by humans and therefore creates many disastrous things that happens to humans and to the planet on which we live. Simply believing that all is pure because all is God, would heal anyone immediately, but how many people actually realize that and truly believe it? The Law of Purity is a powerful law, but it is not a very well observed law. It is a powerful healing energy when it is truly believed and used.

19

UNIVERSAL SPIRITUAL LAW OF BALANCE

The Law of Balance states that each and every aspect of the consciousness of God, from the most infinitesimal, to the most infinite must be in balance with every other aspect. Nothing can displace the Law of Balance. The Law of Balance keeps everything equal. No aspect of the consciousness of God is more important than any other aspect. All are in balance or in relationship to one another, no matter what may appear to human sensitivity.

The Law of Balance is in and of itself one of the most powerful laws. It goes without saying, that things must be in balance, or the universe would cease to exist. Balance, is that perfect point which keeps the physical universe, in order. Balance, is that perfect point which keeps the physical universe moving in the correct way, so that all things are always where they are suppose to be in relation to all other things. They are moving in the direction they must move to keep the steady flow of movement organized, and continuous. If one element of physical creation is out of balance with any other element, utter chaos would exist. Chaos cannot exist in a physical universe for very long. The laws of the physical universe demand that order be established, and balance is the focal point of order. When the physical universe first began, in what is called the "big bang", the release of massive amounts of energy forming into physical matter initially, but very briefly, there was chaos with all physical things, simply moving from their point of origin outward in every direction, but very quickly balance began to be established. Various parts of the huge energy coalesced into physical substance, and began to move itself in ways to be in relationship and balance to other physically evolving substances.

The chaotic period was very short, for physical manifestation will not exist in chaos. Chaos is only natural in the instant of the change from pure energy to physical substance. Once physical substance begins to occur, chaos no longer is, and balance then is the law.

Let's now look at galaxies. All galaxies move in balance with all other galaxies. They maintain the proper distance from one another, they maintain the proper rotation from one another, that they might not collide. They interact with one another in ways that is not detrimental to the life forces that occupy the galaxy. Solar systems, or star systems are the same. Consider, if you will, what would happen if one portion of our star system were to leave our star system. Let us use Jupiter as an example. Should Jupiter somehow be removed from our star system, it would unbalance the entire star system. Its' gravity would be removed and its' presence would be removed. There would be a period of what would seem to be chaotic behavior, as the remaining physical entities, the sun, all of the planets, and the satellites of all of the planets, reorganized themselves to be back in balance with one another without the presence of Jupiter. Balance, then is that which keeps things moving and evolving in the correct fashion with the greatest amount of harmony.

Every physical part of the universe interacts perfectly with every other physical part of the universe. The universe is ever in motion, ever in creation, ever in change and this maintains the balance. There is nothing static in the Law of Balance. The Law of Balance is an active, evolving and changing law in the sense that the Law of Balance changes everything. The law itself is immutable, but the results of the law are constant change. Whole universes physically evolve, and change, and cease to exist in a physical form. As one universe is ceasing to exist in a physical form, other universes are being created into physical form. And the components of the deceased physical universe are going through the change to recreate another physical universe. This is a constant thing, and it is necessary to maintain balance. Since the Infinite Mind is ever creating, there must be change through the Law of Balance that the creation remains in balance.

Our earth does not revolve around the sun as it did hundreds of thousands of years ago. Things have happened to change its rotation and it is a constantly changing thing to maintain balance. Do you remember as a child balancing yourself upon a teeter-totter? While standing in the middle, you had to constantly shift your weight a bit one way, and a bit another way to maintain that balance. It is the same with our solar system. Our solar system is a teeter-totter, and everything in it must be constantly shifting to maintain balance, so that objects do not collide with one another. Occasionally, objects do collide with one another. This does not mean that the Law of Balance is no longer in effect. This means a change is occurring which is necessary in the overall Universal Law of Balance. Not long ago many meteors collided with the planet Jupiter of our solar system. This is of the balance. A change occurred. It did not unbalance the solar system, but it changed every object in our solar system. All objects are now moving slightly differently than they did before this happened. Some people would see this as an act of destruction, especially should such a thing happen upon earth. It is not destruction, it is change, it is part of balance. Things must move and change by the Law of Balance, or balance itself could not be maintained.

Let's look at balance as it applies to the physical and personal. Every human being is a balancing act, and a very admirable balancing act, for the most part. Every atom of your body is constantly balancing itself and every other atom of your body to maintain good health between mind, emotion, soul and body. A healthy body means that all of the organs, atoms, molecules, etc. are in balance. When a body is unhealthy, somewhere the body is out of balance. What causes an out of balance body, is the mind. The mind itself is out of balance. Something is going on within the mind that is creating a lack of balance mentally and something within the spirit is not in balance, thus the physical body becomes unbalanced, ill and suffering. In other words, as I stated earlier, DISEASE IS A REFLECTION OF INTERNAL DYS-EASE. I have learned that this is a very profound and true statement.

When people understand this, they will cease to have physical ailments and they will understand that they must consider the health of their mind, emotions, and spirit. When they consider this, the physical body will be perfect and balanced. Infants are usually born perfectly balanced. Normally, their balance is perfect, every atom perfect, no disease, nothing out of balance. As they are growing, they are picking up the thought patterns, of other people and their perfect balance may be affected and they may become sick and out of balance. That is why it is important that infants be surrounded only by positive and loving thought patterns from the adults and care takers in their surroundings, so that they maintain the natural balance they were born with.

Humans who have become out of balance and are having a physical affect from this lack of balance, must be taught that it is their mind that is causing it. If they can bring their mind into balance, and they can through prayer, meditation, learning, experiencing and surrounding themselves with persons who understand these things, then their body will naturally be brought into balance. The natural state of the physical body is balance. Anything less than balance is a result of improper thinking. This opens the "door" to the onset of imbalance and then disease. The Law of Balance stated very simply would be that all creation is in perfect balance in relation to itself and any flaw in the balance is the result of FLAWED THINKING and can only be corrected by PROPER THINKING. Every human being has the capacity to do this. Some DO it better than others.

When one considers balance, one must look at the principle of interdependency of life forms (animal, vegetable or mineral) on our planet. Due to the very important balance required from that interdependency, one must consider both the long view as well as the short view. Quite often the short term view is based on greed, short sightedness and self gratification which often are very detrimental to the long term view or big picture. Every life form upon our planet is dependent upon every other life form. There is a complete interaction, which is not always visible to human physical consciousness. For instance, humans fail to understand wholly all insect life is valuable, and they attempt to exterminate insect life that they believe is not valuable and that is indeed destructive. This has only resulted in insects which mutate much more rapidly than other life forms, developing a tolerance to the various measures created to destroy them. There is always end of any life form, humans themselves will cease to exist as a specialized life form, many eons from now, but there cannot be complete eradication of one life form by another life form without an absolute and conscious desire to eradicate that life form. This is not conducive to higher evolvement. Rather, it is conducive to the basic consciousness of any life form who attempts such a thing. Humans are even known to have attempted the complete extinction of other types of human being, whom they consider to be inferior.

Certainly, humans have succeeded in eradicating some life forms. Temporarily putting a slight imbalance into effect, but nature, universal law, the Law of Abundance is infinite creativity and it replaces that very quickly with another creation. Whole species have become extinct as a result of the Law of Balance working in ways that humans would call destructive, but is not so. This interdependency then means that humans must learn respect for every life form, must learn to live in balance with every life form, must cease any efforts to eradicate any life form from the planet and must cease the activity which endangers other life forms.

The resources of our planet are great, creativity is infinite, it is however possible to eradicate certain valuable life forms and thus to endanger others. If the deforestation of our planet is carried to its ultimate extreme where there are no more trees, we will seriously endanger every animal life form, which is dependent upon oxygen to live, since the trees provide it. These things are basic understandings that any thinking person should recognize but many do not. The acquisition of objects becomes more important. The short term view is to take whatever the planet offers and use it for human comfort without regard to anything else. That is the short term or competitive activity. The long term is to nurture the resources of our planet, to use them wisely and to give Mother Earth the opportunity to regrow the objects of the surface of her planet and to replace everything that is taken with something of value. If this is done, there will be no deforestation, certain portions will be taken, but quickly replanted so there is continuing forestation, not deforestation. It is quite simple, actually it is the long view rather than the short view.

As the above examples illustrates the importance of balance in all aspects of our life. The balance provides harmony in one's life and in this day and time of daily challenges, pressures and lessons, harmony can be a great comforter. Again one sees how the universal laws are intertwined.

Universal Spiritual Law of Balance and Healing

The Law of Balance is absolutely essential to healing. Balance is a natural healer, even medically speaking. When a person has, for instance, a malignant cancer and it is removed, it restores balance to the body. The surgical removal allows the body to pour its energy into the creation of normal, rather than abnormal cells. All healing depends upon balance. Humans are not always in balance and therefore create disease or even death for themselves. Eventually all will die, but some end their physical expression of life sooner than they should have, because their bodies and their minds are out of balance. The Law of Balance says that everything that exist has a counter to itself, to hold it in balance. The counter, for instance, of sleeping is that you have energy to do things when you awaken. The counter of being awake is that you have sleep to refresh your energy. That is a natural human thing, the balance between sleeping and waking, that the energy might be replenished. There is balance between being hungry and not being hungry. Feelings of hunger result in discomfort because the bodily chemicals are not in balance eating food brings the bodily chemicals back in balance.

There is balance in exercise. The body will become none functional if it is never exercised. Therefore the body naturally goes through exercise when walking, sitting, standing or moving. Even in sleep, the body is constantly moving itself in some way that it might remain strong, rather than become crippled. Persons exercise for strength as well as other things. The body must be exercised to remain functional. Those who become couch potatoes become unhealthy for the body is not getting what it needs. Balance, therefore is a powerful energizer because it provides the body with what it needs to remain healthy or encourages a person to do what is needed to maintain health and when not in perfect health to get the proper treatment. This also applies to mental health. Balance is the very core of mental stability. A mentally well balanced person is not going to become schizophrenic, paranoid or etc. as long as balance remains. When a person becomes mentally out of balance, they are no longer able to think clearly, and are diagnosed with various mental illnesses, but the real cause of mental illness is lack of the healing power of balance. This is why it is so important for parents to provide a balanced attitude toward their children, not becoming violently angry one moment and then hugging them the next. Children react to unbalanced attitudes, thoughts, and deeds of adults. A well balanced adult applies discipline as needed, but applies love all the time.

Now we come to the crux of the Law of Balance. There is only one energy that balances everything all the time and that is the energy of love. Love is the only perfect balance in the entire universe. All balance is achieved through love, or it is not true balance. Persons who do not love themselves are in a state of imbalance. Only loving oneself as the perfect child of God can create the necessary balance. Persons who do not love other persons are unbalanced mentally, and only love can heal them. Persons who do not love themselves become physically ill for the body responds to the mental imbalance. Any act, word or deed that is less than loving, produces chemicals in the physical body that if not corrected, will lead to physical, mental or emotional lack of well-being. Thus for balance to exist, love much exist. Acts of violence are not balancing acts. For instance, when there is religious warfare. This is totally out of balance, and causes great agony and distress and it causes very negative Karma. For the persons fighting, there is no love, there is only prejudice, hatred, and determination. These are not aspects of balance. Balance does not permit hatred, for hatred throws balance out. That which is not love, cannot work in the Law of Balance except negatively. If you perceive that your angry thoughts create an infection in the body, yes you can perceive that this is the Law of Balance in action. For negativity creates negativity. The Law of Balance is one of the most powerful aspect of healing, but most people do not perceive it so because they do not understand the law. When persons understand what is stated above, hopefully they will seek to keep a balanced lifestyle as loving as possible and free of negativity as possible, so that they might be in fullest power of the Law of Balance and remain mentally, emotionally spiritually and physically healthy. If they do falter, they will at least know how to bring healing in by bringing balance in, by changing the thought pattern, balancing through the act and thought of love.

Comments/Examples Law of Balance

Let us speak for a moment on medical healing and true healing. Medical healing is a fine and wonderful thing and it has served a valuable and useful purpose in the current conditions of humanity, and the other life forms upon our planet. It is a result of intellect and intuition combining to create healing methods that we in our present state of evolution are able to understand and relate to. All medical healing is good and positive, and must be continued. However there will come a time when the practice of medicine will be very different than it is today and when the machines that have been created will be less necessary or unnecessary. By the time these machines are obsolete, humanity will be reaching for other ways of healing. Many humans already are using alternative healing methods, combing spiritual and the medical, or purely spiritual healing methods. Thus, again the Law of Balance will be offered here. There is balance between what you have and what you need, and what you will continue to need. If what you need changes, and a different balance comes into affect, what you require will be available to you.

As the art of true inner healing expands and is more recognized and accepted, there will still be persons who will simply not be able to heal themselves and they will require the services of healers of various kinds. The healing profession will change, but the art of healing will still remain among the noblest of human activities. In the Law of Balance, persons are often more able to help others than to help themselves, and thus the healing practice will unlikely to ever become completely self-healing.

As I have told many of my patients with "tongue in cheek" not to reveal the true secrets of healing as I give it to them. That is that, all true healing comes from within. Doctors don't truly heal people.

Our job is to help people heal themselves. This can be accomplished in many ways such as: providing insight to their disease and dys-ease, medication, surgery, help them change their thinking and actions in many other ways. Healers for the most part are facilitators. Such facilitators will continue to be needed. Part of the facilitation will be in the teaching of methods of self-healing. Rather than the facilitator being the one to provide information that will make self-healing more easily accomplished, but as I have pointed out, it is unlikely that for a number of centuries, complete self-healing will be acquired by all life forms upon our planet.

Even though we human life forms feel we are the most evolved, there are numerous "lower life forms" with greater healing abilities. These life forms can be cut in half or loose major appendages and they will regrow a completely new body part to replace the one lost. They are simply guided by Mother Nature, where as we often "fight" Mother Nature. By using the Universal Spiritual Laws in harmony and balance we will achieve what is now thought of as the impossible.

20

UNIVERSAL SPIRITUAL LAW OF PATIENCE

The law of Patience simply stated is that all things are created in the exact perfect length of time required for their perfect creation. Patience is creation in action. Impatience greatly lengthens the perfect time to create a desired result. The more patience is acquired, the more is created, the more impatience an individual is, the less creative that individual will be, and the longer it will take to create the given desired end. Impatience creates one thing superbly, and that is obstacles to the desired goal. Impatience is a highly creative emotion, unfortunately it creates exactly what you do not want. It is thus, a perversion of the laws that govern creation, or I should say a seeming perversion, there is not perversion of the laws of Creation. If you wish to accomplish something, and you become impatient, then what you create is one obstacle after another which may lead to frustration, anger and greater impatience, which adds to the length of time, and which may cause considerable difficulty for yourself. You may, in your impatience to hang a picture for instance begin to hammer into your wall without sufficient preparation, because you are impatient to complete the job and hammer a portion not supported, and instead of a nail hole, create a very large hole in your wall. You may hit your own finger, rather than the nail you are attempting to place in a given area. These are results of impatience which only creates obstacles. Patience, on the other hand, creates the desired result perfectly in the perfect amount of time to complete the project and to be pleased with the results.

The Law of Patience is perhaps the one most humans have the greatest difficulty with. You do not even need to consider humanity in this, for the Law of Patience governs the universe by the fact that part of the essence of the universe itself is pure patience. The universe cares not whether it takes a single second or a thousand billion years to complete a given aspect of its creativity. The universe then is created in patience. There is no hurry, no time frame, without patience the universe would be less than pure, less than perfect, and it is perfect. Patience is that aspect of Universal Law which proceeds exactly according to guidelines, to plans, to needs in creating the perfect universe and keeping the creation going. As humans enter into Aquarian consciousness, they will begin to understand more fully the Law of Patience and more and more will begin to achieve it. As humans truly understand that they are part of universal creation, patience becomes a natural aspect of human consciousness. Without patience, again there could be no creation.

Let us speak of impatience and patience both as the emotions that they are. Emotions, is that which makes something happen, it is energy. Patience is a very fine emotional energy to have. It allows you to enjoy the fruits of your patient creations. Impatience is mostly a destructive emotion. It is energy used to destroy that which you most wish to create. An example would be young people governed by their passions and emotions, not knowing how to govern their emotions and master them. They give into the energy of the moment and engage in sexual activity which may result in an unwanted pregnancy, certain sexually transmitted disease and social ostracization. Immature young people giving birth to babies and young men are often not being responsible for the results of their sexual activity. Patience, on the other hand would guide these young people to master the emotions and passions of their hormones and to desire to wait until they are in a position to commit themselves to one another, to care for the product of their love, their infant, to govern themselves and to be productive members of society. Impatience leads to consequences which often one must live with for the rest of their lives. Patience also leads to consequences which one may have to live with for the rest of their lives . But the consequences are diametrically opposite. Patience leads to young people becoming mature, educated, ready for a true commitment to one another, ready to care for, nurture the children who come of their love. Impatience obviously promotes the exact opposite consequences.

One of the reasons that humans are so impatient is that mankind is a very young race. Our planet is a young planet. Naturally, the life forms of our planets must be young. Humans are in infancy, really in many ways, likewise the two year old is very impatient and given to temper tantrums of screaming when it cannot have instant gratification. In many ways the entire human race is like a two year old demanding instant gratification and having temper tantrums when it does not acquire its' desired goal instantly. It is understandable then, that about 75% of humans upon this earth, are here to learn to be patient, to master impatience and mutate it and transmute it into patience. We will eventually acquire patience. Ways to acquire it include prayer, meditation, demanding of yourself that you consciously act in patient ways and giving yourself daily goals to provide you with opportunities to be patient. A simple example is the placing of a nail in a wall to hang a picture. You would take the time to test your wall to find the place where there is support, get the proper tools and line them up to measure correctly so that your nail will go in where you wish it to, and the place where the picture will be hung will be in balance with other objects in your room. This might take a while, but you would be consciously working towards patience, and when the nail was finally in the perfect place, the picture would be hung perfectly. You would have created a perfect result in the perfect length of time necessary for that creation. You would be satisfied with your creation, you would admire it and enjoy it. If daily you would give yourself an attainable goal that you will work to attain, for that day or however long it is, this would be consciously working with the Law of Patience to retain more of it for yourself. In your meditation do not set yourself a time limit, be patient and take as long as you feel comfortable. When you are no longer comfortable mentally, emotionally and physically, you have spent the perfect time length for meditation. It might be one second, it might be an hour, it might be a day, a week, whatever. Setting time limits encourages impatience, giving one's self no limitations encourages patience. Impatience limits one, patience makes one utterly limitless. In our current society it is often necessary to set time limitations, unfortunately. When you do not have pressure upon you, do not limit your time and allow yourself to consciously realize that you are working towards the acquisition of patience. Then let yourself drift into a meditative prayerful state, and allow no limitations to be placed upon you. Patience is absolutely necessary for good creation. Many persons practice patience in some parts of their life, but not in other parts.

Particularly in this day and time, parenting is an excellent opportunity for learning and practicing the lessons of patience. If you demonstrate patience to your children, if you treat them with respect and do not become impatient when they cannot immediately or quickly do what you want them to, then you teach by example that patience is a virtue. Thus, hopefully your children will grow up to do the same and treat their families in the same way.

Your children must be taught to be more patient. Who better to teach them than their parents whom they love and respect, and would wish to follow in your footsteps. Young children mimic their parents and other adults. Who else do they have to follow? Your example to your sons and daughters will be the biggest gift than you can give them. I repeat again, patience is a gift beyond value, for without it, little constructive or good can be accomplished. With it, all things are possible.

Universal Spiritual Law of Patience and Healing

Patience is one of the most difficult laws for most people to follow. At any given time of the people who have come into this life to learn patience are doing very well. Patience properly learned can keep disease away from a person completely. They do not attract disease to them when they have truly learned patience. If they have not yet learned patience and have attracted a disease to themselves through impatience thinking, or impatience acting or impatient words, by achieving something of patience they can put positive health energy into the situation and thus heal themselves.

Patience then is vital to human health in more ways than one. Millions of persons have died for lack of patience, in accidents that would not have happened had they been patience. Also in wars that should not have happened, but happened because one side or the other lost patience and decided to act rather than continue attempting to resolve their differences in a patient fashion. Impatience then creates nothing but unwelcomed consequences. Patience on the other hand, creates very welcomed consequences. Things that persons may choose to do, if they patiently work at them come about more rapidly and with greater harmony. The interesting thing about patience is this, when a person is patient, they achieve what they want more rapidly for patience is a pure love energy, a highly creative energy. Therefore patient persons have a higher level of energy, they think more clearly, thus they are able to create more effectively and to achieve a desired goal more rapidly. People who are impatient, are by the very energy of impatience, creating obstacles. For one thing, they do not think correctly, for impatience muddles the thinking process. Thus they can not think of what they wish to do in a creative way, but only in a frustrated way. Their body reacts to this by becoming unhealthy. An impatience person will frequently make dreadful mistakes and have to begin all over again with a project. Where a patient person will take it step by step and do it correctly the first time.

Impatience then, creates mental, emotional, physical, and spiritual dys-ease. Patience creates healthy thoughts, words, deeds, and responses. Patience, when it finally arrives as it must in every situation, immediately begins the healing process for that of which is caused by lack of patience. It thus makes sense to work very hard being patient, knowing that it makes things happen sooner. What one with patience can achieve in let us say a year, if impatience settles in, it could easily take five years or ten years or never be accomplished at all, for the mind would not be able to perceive how to accomplish it.

Patience should be considered not only one of the highest aspect of love and one of the most powerful healing energy, so it should be considered essential to human survival. As for instance, impatiently, humans are slaughtering the equatorial rain forest. Their impatience to plant things leads them to deeds that will eventually result in the death of many humans, who otherwise would have lived long and productive lives. There are many plant life forms whose essence is healing, that are being destroyed and they cannot be replaced. Impatience then, could if carried to its fullest extent, result in the disappearance of humans from planet earth, while still leaving other life forms, plants and animals, to exist on our beautiful planet earth. Only patience can stop humanity from acting self-destructive. Patience is a healer, and a creator. Impatience is neither of these.

Do not be confused by the saying, "All things come to those who wait". There must be a balance between patience and getting the job done. But you can't just sit there and think nice thoughts and expect to achieve your goals. Patience does require action. Of course, you must get out there and do what you need to do to the best of your ability. The Law of Patience does not suggest that you just sit still and expect things to come to you, but rather being patient in your approach. Do not try to do everything at once. Make a reasonable goal and work toward the goal. Do not expect that the goal will come to you. An example of how impatience manifests itself is when impatient people frequently do very inappropriate things, such as not giving themselves sufficient time to arrive where they need to be and thus must walk, drive or run recklessly and injuring or endangering themselves and others. Most really impatient people are that way because they do not know anything about time management. They try to cram too much into a small period of time, becoming impatient when they cannot get it all done or they act in lazy ways for a while and then try to get everything done in half the time it should actual take. Persons who are patient are generally people who are thinking. They are planning things and working towards things that may or may not manifest. I am not the most patient person, but I have had to be patient in my spiritual path toward learning the real Truths of our Universe and putting them to work in my life and professional medical work and writing. It has taken many years and I feel with the loving help of Spirit, I have been able to create a far better birth and healing experience as well as help people understand how to live the life God meant us to live. To be goal oriented is good but you should also be willing to work toward your goals in a patient way, so that you will achieve the full goal, not some impatiently constructed goal that really does not even meet your first desire. Impatient people try to do something before they really know what they are doing.

So simply put: Patience is a virtue.

UNIVERSAL SPIRITUAL LAW OF CREATION

21

The Law of Creation is the law that says "I am, therefore I create". No aspect of the consciousness of God can fail to follow the Law of Creation. It is a natural law, so profound that it is impossible to even attempt to break or circumvent it. The universe is a conscious thing and consciousness means creation. The Law of Creation then is more than just making something, it is a major part of self-awareness. The universe is, infinitely creating, and every aspect of the Universal Consciousness is constantly creating because it cannot fail to do so. All creation begins with love even that which becomes distorted in the process, begins with love. There is no creation without the Law of Love. The Law of Creation simply states that love, in its infinite state is infinitely creative. Creation must exist and creation is constantly changing. New things are being created, things that have been created are recreated. Things that have been created, cease to exist in their current forms, but creation continues. Infinite intelligence is incapable of non-creation. Entire universes are constantly being created and recreated. Everything that is, is creation, whether it is spiritual or physical, it is creation in action. Creation is thought in action, for infinite intelligence is constantly and eternally thinking and every thought produces creation. Thought itself is creation, the results of thought is creation. You create by every thought. Creation is infinite, eternal, and unable to cease.

It is very important to understand that the first step in creation is thought. Without thought there is not creation and without creation there is not thought. Not every thought leads to a specific creation but all creation starts with thought and if the energy and effort is strong enough and persists, then the creation will result. Most people seem to not realize how powerful thought can be and seem to view thought as quite often just an activity without effects or consequences.

Thoughts are energy which can be registered by sophisticated medical equipment. This thought energy is initiated by the human mind and the energy waves go out into the universe where they have potential to join with other thoughts and energy and create. The creation can have a positive or negative affect depending upon the type of original thought. It is like throwing a rock into a pond and seeing the ripples that are created by the rock (thought) and seeing how they propagate in all directions and affect things in their path. One needs to know the power of the thought process and begin to take responsibility for their thoughts and what they may create. So consciously work on your thought process so that you send out positive loving thoughts because as we have previously learned, thoughts and acts come back to you and often in multiplied form. Again, we see the interaction of the laws of the universe. We will talk more about this in a later law (prayer, meditation and thought). That which is physical cannot be permanent. That which is spiritual is permanent, but it is always changing. That which is physical cannot be permanent because nothing physical has the strength to be a permanent creation, for physical strength is not a permanent thing. Strength is a permanent thing, but not physical strength. Thus, every facet of physical creation ceases to exist by one means or another in its current state. It is always changing its state, but eventually its' state ceases to exist, and that which has been, forms the raw substance for other physical creations. This is an observable phenomenon upon earth. A flower dies, its physical being no longer exists, but the seeds it has passed exist and will create other flowers, simple but effective. Creation goes on, but physical aspect of creation cease to exist in their current form in due time.

I believe that the analogy of the flower, above, demonstrates that nothing is wasted in creation. Not only does its seeds continue, but the flower itself becomes fertilizer for other physical expressions of life. let us take something more far reaching as a rule that nothing is wasted. Millions of years ago, life forms existed upon our planet called dinosaurs. A catastrophe came which made our earth's atmosphere incompatible with dinosaurs and they died. It is called, as our scientist have speculated a combination of events, one of which was a bombardment of other physical objects from our solar system which created an ice age, by darkening the atmosphere around our planet, so that the rays of the sun were not sufficient to maintain the dinosaur life form, for it required more heat than other life forms. These giant beasts, and the vegetable life forms who required greater heat then was obtainable, died and decayed. Various things happened that covered these remains of life forms with great amounts of earth, and in their decaying state they were essentially, through the laws of change, balance and of creation, changed into oil and petroleum, products that we now use for many purposes. That is a huge example on our own planet of how nothing is wasted. A life form ceased to exist in its own form, but created a vast reservoir of useable energy. Nothing is ever wasted.

Now let us look at a more practical aspect of the use of the Law of Creation and in order to create more abundance in one's life. We begin with other laws than the Law of Creation. We begin, first of all with the Law of Love. Do you love yourself enough that you believe that you deserve grater abundance in your life? You must first determine that. This brings in the Law of Patience. You must patiently examine your own feelings for yourself, not only your conscious feelings, but you must go into your subconscious through meditation to discover how much you love yourself, how deserving you believe you are. This will involve much patience for the first response of humans is to say, of course I deserve it. If you really love yourself and believe you deserve it, you will obtain it. If you are not obtaining it, it is because your impatience has caused you to neglect the proper steps. Having ascertained what areas you may not be loving yourself sufficiently in, you will put effort into loving yourself more fully, more patience is involved here. This may take awhile, it may not be done immediately. You may not have instantaneous feeling of the self-love experience. The Law of Patience comes in, the Law of Abundance is a natural part of the Law of Love, the Law of Balance and the Law of Patience. Once you have patiently worked out your feelings of deserving the abundance you desire, you are now ready to do the work to acquire the abundance. You will patiently meditate, seeking answers as to how you may bring greater abundance in the form of monetary income into your life. You will be inspired to do certain things. Intuitively, you will find that certain thought patterns, that come to you, have great possibility. You will patiently follow-up on each of these possibilities. Each of them will show themselves to be good, and working with all of them you will find that they work well together.

This outline is safe to follow and must result in greater monetary abundance, for you have followed Divine Law.

I would say that the two most important laws involved in acquiring abundance are the Law of Love, loving yourself, and the Law of Patience. If you follow these laws, the Law of Abundance is a natural consequence. This is your outline. love yourself, patiently examine any lack of love and correct it. Patiently seek guidance in how to put the law of Abundance into effect in your life, now that you know you deserve it. Use your intuition to create abundance for yourself because the Law of Abundance says you must. You have then followed these laws, and the Law of Creation inevitably brings to you the result of your faithful following of the other laws. They do not work alone, they all work together.

It is not enough just to love yourself. That does not automatically create abundance, it is not even enough to be patient, you must also be creative. You must know that abundance is limitless and creation is your natural ability. When you work all of the laws together, they work well. When you try to work one only, you are leaving something out of your creation, and the Law of Creation only works when it is correctly applied. This again illustrates the interdependence and the importance if all the laws which stem from the Law of Love.

When one learns this and truly puts it into action by instigating interaction at a constant level with the Law of Love, your own loving creativity will guide you to the use of all the other laws in highly creative ways.

Things bring us to what is called the Universal Law Equation, which is truly quite simple, as previously stated: "God is One, One is All and All is God". It can also be stated thusly, "Infinite Intelligence is One, One is All". Again illustrating that when one wants to properly use and apply universal law they are used in concert with each other.

Universal Spiritual Law of Creation and Healing

The Law of Creation is somewhat of a summary kind of law, for what is the ultimate result of every thought? You cannot think a thought without creation happening. Creation is a law that brings in results because creation is results. That which is created is the result of first a thought, then when necessary a word, a deed, and all the other things that are required to create something. It is interesting that the Law of Creation is both a universal law and the result of its own being. Everything is created. All that is, is creation. Thus the Law of Creation both exists and exists because it is proving itself. It is the net result of itself. When you think a thought, that is the Law of Creation. When you act upon the thought, that is the Law of Creation and so on, until that which you have thought becomes reality, at least to you and frequently to other people. Everything that is, is of the Law of Creation. It is hard to explain it, but that it is the way it is. You create what you think. Now creative thought both creates healthy conditions and creates the energy necessary to heal unhealthy conditions. Therefore the Law of Creation is constantly repeating itself, but every repetition of the law is in some way different than any other creation or thought. Every thought is unique. Every thought is different than every other thought. Therefore every creation, in some way is different from any other creation, for it manifested from a different thought. Two people may both think at the very same time "I am Love" but they will think it differently according to their own perception of love. Therefore that which is created from the thought will be different. It will still be a creation of love but it will not be exactly the same creation. Thus it behooves all persons to think loving, creative thoughts, and to know they have the power to create a perfectly healthy body, mind and spirit and if it is not yet healthy, to heal it of the results of negative thought patterns into a healthy body. Humans have the right to heal any life form though loving creative thoughts, but they do not have the right to destroy any life forms. That is a different kind of creativity. The Law of Creation is not the law of destruction. They are very different points of view. There is no law of destruction, but often times humans act as if there were. Humans have a responsibility to every life form, for every life form is the result of creative thinking by the great mind of the universe called God. Thus the Law of Creation simply stated says, WHAT YOU THINK, YOU CREATE. If you are to create positively you must think positively. You think yourself healthy and you think yourself unhealthy, you choose.

UNIVERSAL SPIRITUAL LAW OF PRAYER, MEDITATION AND THOUGHT

22

These laws are not specifically great laws by themselves, but the understanding of them will help individuals understand more fully all of universal law. The purpose of these particular laws is to insure that all individuals, whatever the state of their spiritual progression, whatever their philosophical belief, whatever their religious or spiritual leanings would have a greater ability to work fully within all of the laws.

These three forms of mental and spiritual activity are very closely interrelated as one would expect. Prayer is the most powerful thought form because true prayer is solute love in thought form. All of creation prays, whether knowingly or unknowingly. Prayer incorporates all of natural law. Prayer is an act of creation. The purpose of prayer is to create, and in and of itself creates whatever is the desired objective. This is why it is so important to meditate upon whether or not you truly wish to pray for a certain desired result, because prayer is creation put into powerful action. Prayer consists of three parts, the law of prayer is thus: Asking, Affirming, Giving Thanks in any order. When one wishes to pray, one should have previously sought counsel as to whether the thing they are praying for is truly in their soul's best progression. This, what I am now about to say, may sound a contradiction, for I say to you that before one meditates one should pray, but it is not. For instance, when you go into acting within the Law of Meditation, and that law states that you must receive answers to your questions, solutions to your challenges, information that will enable you to direct your life upon the pathway it chooses to take, but before you meditate you must pray, and before you pray you must meditate.

It works thus, when you meditate today, you will first ask that you receive whatever information is of value to you. You will affirm the information is available and you will give thanks that the information will be received. You will then enter into quiet meditation, and what you receive at that time you will make note of, you will act upon, you will then end the meditation with a prayer. More about this later.

Returning to prayer we find that in their own way all life forms use prayer, although they may call it by many different names. It is a direct communication with the Essence of God, it is therefore entirely correct to say that when an individual prays, they are in essence praying to themselves and to all other life forms. Remember, All is God. You are therefore to understand that you are not directing your prayer to an individual being, somewhere in the universe who may or may not hear the prayer, and may or may not answer the prayer. You are directing your prayer toward all life forms in the universe. Your thought pattern called, prayer, then is being in some way, received, whether consciously or unconsciously by every atom of the universe, including yourself. With this much power available, it is no wonder that prayer is the most powerful thought form, for it is all inclusive. When you ask for something in prayer, you are directing the entire universe, every atom of the universe, to assist you in the creation of what you desire or need in your particular life pattern.

Perhaps, if everyone understood this, more persons would find that their prayers are answered in ways that are understandable to them. All prayer is answered, it is not always, however answered in ways that are understandable. When you deliver thought form, every atom of the universe is working to achieve that which you're praying for. When you take into consideration that countless billions of thought forms are also involved in their own prayer activities, you begin to understand more of the Law of Motion, for prayer is motion, it makes things happen. Prayer is creativity, it makes things happen. It is powerful beyond ones' ability to comprehend. Most persons think of prayer as something that is directed for a specific need, for instance you pray for health, for abundance, for a loving relationship, for the resolution of certain challenges in your life pattern. Prayer is far beyond that. You may be specific, and the specific answers come to you, but every prayer is also generalized, for basically most life forms will be praying for much the same thing. Every life forms desires to be healthy, happy, abundant and successful in their relationships. These are normal prayer, therefore the universe is constantly in powerful action to bring to every life form, those natural needs that must be satisfied, if the life form is to live in harmony.

Most persons think of prayer, then as a beneficial and a somewhat benign activity. It is indeed beneficial, it is far from benign, it is very very powerful. Also, we must recognize that there are persons who pray for things that are less than beneficial, their prayers are equally powerful. It is not that there is opposition between what is truly beneficial, and that which is not, for prayers are active, no matter which way the prayer is directed. It is energy in action and in movement. Most persons do not deliberately pray, for that which would be harmful, but they do not recognize that what they are praying for has the potential to be harmful to themselves, or to others. This is why, sometimes when prayer is answered, persons are less than happy with the results that are achieved in their life. They have received all or a portion of what they have prayed for, and it proves not to be that which they need and use and will find truly beneficial in their life's experience.

I will give you a very broad example of this. Some years ago a group of individuals in Germany came to the conclusion that their particular genotype was superior to all other genotypes, and it would be a good, beneficial, and righteous thing for them to remove from the earth certain genotypes that they found offensive. To them, this was good, it was righteous, it was even thought to be directed by God, that they should do this thing. Their prayers were fervent. To them, their desires were righteous, and God ordained, and through their prayer, their work, they created a situation designated World War II. They were not inherently evil, they were misdirected in the areas in which their energies should have been used. For a period of time it seemed that their prayers were being answered as they successfully invaded and conquered many countries surrounding them, and began their program of eliminating those whom they believed should not share the planet with them. They felt righteous, they felt in control, they felt that God was on their side and their prayers were answered. It became apparent as time passed that while their prayers were answered, they were not right, they were not what you would term correct thinking and thus the grand plan that they had conceived and prayed for, ended in utter humiliating defeat for them. This is a very common thing.

Most people do not know how to pray successfully. They pray for what they perceive to be the best thing. This, then leads us to the need for meditation. Meditation is the other side of the coin. In prayer, one's powerful thoughts go forth designating certain desires and goals. The energy is put into action, things happen, the universe responds, God is working, and things begin to occur that seem to be the answer to the prayer and they are the answer to the prayers. Meditation is asking for guidance. If a person asks for guidance they may discover that what they are considering to pray for is not in their best behalf. The two are inseparable, prayer and meditation. Two sides of the same coin, but they must be understood and correctly used. Simply put, prayer is asking for specific things, meditation is receiving specific answers, and using the guidance to help in what you pray for. Therefore, the correct way to use prayer and meditation is quite simple. When one places themselves in a meditative and prayerful frame of mind they would wisely pray: "I ask now that that which is for my best good, my greatest progression, and the loving and harmonious solution to my challenges be given to me". Then, the meditation would go into effect, in which quietly there is listening, accepting learning to understand the direction that is given. Intuition comes into play at this time. For all humans have intuition, with some, it is more intense than others, for those who have achieved the ability to see and hear at the psychic level, there will be suggestions given, pictures will be shown, voices will be heard, a mental note will be made on the part of the individual to remember and use information thus gleamed. At the end of the meditation session the person is then able to know what specifically to pray for and the meditation session turns back in to prayer in which specific prayers may be offered, and of course always a thank you for the session in that the prayer is already answered, even if you do not have the solution as yet. Prayer consists of asking, affirming and thanking. Meditation consists of receiving, you may use these things in any order but wisely before meditating you would ask that your meditation give you the information necessary for powerful prayer to go forth.

Using prayer and meditation this way, you know what you are praying for, you know that it will be righteous and pure, and it will benefit you and thus benefit everyone associated with you, and in fact benefit the entire universe.

Always pray for that which is beneficial to everyone, for if it is truly beneficial to you, it will be. This is where Germans made their basic mistake, which led to the great tragedies that followed. They prayed only for that which they firmly believed would benefit them, and did not consider whether it benefited anyone else or not. Prayer must benefit all, or it is misdirected prayer, and it is a use of the energy of prayer in ways that ended up not even benefiting the petitioner. Thus, you can see how these two things, prayer and meditation interact with every other law to maintain harmony and equilibrium in the universe.

Thought, of course is not a law unto itself, it is part of everything that exists, it is impossible not to think. Every life form is constantly thinking. The idea is to learn what you are thinking so that if you are thinking things that are not of benefit to you, and to other life-forms, you will cease to do so. Thought creates. Every thought instantly begins to create a result. Persons who have evolved to the point where they have absolute mastery over their thoughts learn to think only in beneficial ways. This requires many lifetimes and must find sense in spirit between lifetimes. Any individual can consciously begin to do this.

For instance, a situation may arise in which your first thought is one of anger and dislike for another person who has treated you in a callous or unhappy fashion. Your thought may be of anger, and you wish to do something in retaliation to that individual. When you have begun to learn the principles of personal thought control, the instant you think an angry thought toward another person, no matter what has motivated it, you will recognize what you are doing, will stop that thought form, and instead project love to the individual.

You will forgive yourself for the thought form that you have been projecting and you will transmute that thought formed into love. This is not a denigration of humanity, it is simply a recognition that this is a process that is not easily attained. There are, however many millions who are beginning to recognize when they are having a thought that is not truly beneficial, and are beginning to change those thoughts, to ask for and receive personal forgiveness. Who forgives you? You forgive you- for you are God. The universe forgives you- for the universe is God. When you ask forgiveness it is granted instantly. As humans become more aware of the power of thought in the Aquarian Age, they will choose to monitor their thoughts, all will be working toward that desirable goal. Thought then is creation. Prayer, meditation and thought are all things in creative activity.

Universal Spiritual Law of Prayer, Meditation and Thought and Healing

In every real sense all loving thoughts are a form of prayer. Loving thoughts are profound healing energy. For instance, to hold a child in your arms and only think of how I love this child, I would do anything for it and it is the most important person in the world to me. It is a healing energy that touches not only the child but it works throughout the chemical system of the adult body to bring extra healing, extra energy, and the foundation for continuing thoughts of love. A thought is a powerful thing. It creates, sometimes instantly. As a result, thought and prayer are so closely aligned that we must consider every loving thought a form of prayer and is healing in action. The same is true of meditation. Meditation is a time of quiet listening, a time of being aware of ones' own self, one's own thoughts and of opening oneself up to the universal thought pattern. We speak not only of the spirit energy and their thoughts coming to the human body but the universe itself, for as we know, the universe is full of thought. Everything that has ever been thought, by any life form, is permanently within the Universal Mind or the Universal thought pattern. Thus the thoughts that occur during meditation, whether one is going within to commune with one's own highest level of consciousness or one is seeking the thought pattern of another life form to gain information, healing or consolation. The thought, if they are offered in love by the person meditating or by life forms responding to the meditation, are by their very nature of being loving, is healing energy.

When one works with spirit, they talk to you, heal you, help you, guide you and council you. But there is also the other side of the coin, their thoughts are just as healing to them as they are to you. When spirits are offering you love during your times of meditation or at any other time, they are also being healed. When they work with a newly arrived spirit on the other side, praying for their healing of every kind, sending them thoughts of love, they are also receiving healing themselves. People do not think of spirit or angels as needing healing, but all life forms respond to loving prayer, loving meditation and the thoughts they have and respond to the thoughts they receive.

Prayer is the single most powerful thought form in the entire universe and as prayer it almost always follows a thought of love. It is healing to the person who is praying, it is healing to the person who receives the prayer and it sends healing into the entire universe, so that every life form may benefit from the thought of one life form. All loving thoughts are prayer in action, in one form or another. Spirit has observed that most humans pray more often for others than they do for themselves. This leads them to the conclusion that the natural human consciousness is one of giving and one of serving. The exception, when one is angry, is not healing. One should pray every day for their own health and well-being, as well as for the health and well-being for others. The highest consciousness of humans is evident in prayer, for it is often a very private thing for many people. The majority of humans, pray in some way every day. There is much more prayer activity prevalent in human thought form than most humans recognize and prayer is instantly healing even though the result of the prayer may not always show themselves immediately. The healing immediately begins and the person who is offering the prayer is immediately uplifted and healing begins to occur.

Meditation and prayer are two sides of the same coin. It is correctly stated that prayer is speaking of one's needs, one's gratitude and one's desires. Meditation is the quiet that allows the loving thoughts of self or other life forms to enter in and help to achieve the desire goals.

The most powerful prayer form is gratitude. When thanks are given in prayer, the power increases many fold. That is why spirit often encourages people to begin a prayer with thanks rather than asking for what is desired or needed. Affirmations are very powerful in prayer. To affirm that the prayer is even now being answered, is a powerful statement of faith, not only in God, but in one's own self. Asking in prayer for one's needs, helps the individual to categorize and to think more clearly and clear thought naturally brings about healing. Surely your spirit guides and teachers and the Universal Mind of God knows your needs and desires and what is required for you to be a happy and productive person, but your prayers are still needed. Often people will pray in desperation "God help me". They do not even know what they need. There may be great confusion in their mind, but that simple prayer, "God help me'" creates a healing energy and thought process that enables them to then more clearly understand what the help is that they require. Just that understanding alone, brings a sense of relief and gratitude. Then comes the words of thanks or thoughts of thanks. Then will come, either immediately or shortly there after, the affirmation that the work is now in progress and the result will be correct for all involved. Thought, meditation and prayer are, in a very real sense a dynamic trio of accomplishment and of absolute healing. You cannot pray without healing occurring, even if you are not specifically asking for healing for yourself or another. The moment you enter into the thought mode that is called prayer, healing begins. It refreshes and energizes the physical body, opens the human mind and soul to expansion of consciousness to higher thought patterns for all the things that are necessary for a healthy body, mind, emotion, soul and spirit. Thus in conclusion, remember every loving thought is prayer in action, so have many of them each day of your life.

I'm sure when some or many people read about prayers being answered they will say, "Well, when my friend or family member got sick or injured, I prayed for them and they didn't get any better or they even got worse". Why did that happen, instead of my prayers along with others being answered and the person being healed. You said, "As soon as you pray healing begins immediately".

These are not difficult questions to answer. We may pray for other people, but it is that person's choice whether or not they wish to allow the healing to happen. Healing immediately begins to happen in the person creating the prayer. The energy of healing is offered to the person for whom one is praying, but it is their choice, whether consciously or subconsciously, to accept the healing. That is also a form of healing, for they have made a decision to go another pathway whether they are aware of it or not. If there has been confusion in mind, it can be removed by the decision that they make. Decisions are made at every level of consciousness. Prayer catches every level of consciousness, but we can not subvert in any way, the absolute right of freedom of choice upon the part of every life form. So prayer, thought and meditation are of great power and will serve you well. Work on your techniques for them and use them often.

UNIVERSAL SPIRITUAL LAW OF MOTION

23

The Law of Motion is a part of what enables the universe to continue and obviously keeps things moving. Everything, every aspect of creation, is in constant motion. The Law of Motion states that which moves is constantly creating and all things are constantly moving, thus constantly creating. Nothing is even at rest, even when it seems to be. Without motion nothing would happen. Every atom, molecule and particle of the universe is in constant motion. There is never a cessation of motion. Love is energy in motion. It is the Law of Love that creates motion which then becomes a law unto itself. Motion is so powerful a law and activity, that there is no way that anything can cause motion to cease. This is more easily described in scientific terms that in metaphysical terms because it is a universal law that is easy to observe. For example, you sit quietly, you attempt to not move a single muscle of your body, but you know that your body is in constant motion, whether you are moving it in ways that you are able to see or not. The body can be in complete repose, and yet it is in constant activity, every blood cell moving, every organ moving and breathing is motion. There is no way that motion can cease. Our planet is in motion, in and of itself as it moves upon its axis and rotates in harmony with the other planets of our solar system.

Every atom that composes the planet earth is in constant motion, the Law of Motion is to be called the very Law of Existence. If anything could cease to be in motion it would cease to exist, and nothing ever ceases to exist. When your physical body no longer holds your spirit, it will not be animated in the sense that you can move it, can walk with it, talk through it, but it will be in constant motion. Every atom of the body will continue to be in motion. As the decay of the body sets in, immense amounts of energy are released, the body is still an active, moving thing. It is moving in different ways than it did when the spirit was within it. As the atoms decay, that energy creates other life forms. The body remains in action until it has completely changed its structure to provide nourishment for other life forms. It is then no longer a single unit of motion and activity. It is a part of all motion and activity throughout the universe, and from that motion and activity, other life forms come into physical existence. Nothing ever stops moving, it simply moves in other ways.

Universal Spiritual Law of Motion and Healing

The Law of Motion is such a simple yet elegant law of the universe. Everything is always in motion. Nothing is static. Motion itself is healing. Your body is inwardly in motion even if you are motionless. In prayer and meditation the heart is beating, the blood is circulating, the chemical secretions are being properly secreted, the body is digesting and preparing to utilize the food energy that it has taken in. If medication has been taken, the inward motion of the body absorbed the virtue of the medication and eliminated the residue through the Law of Motion. Motion is healing in physical action. A healthy body is always creating motion that is healing. A diseased body is creating motion that will be healing, for the body is naturally inclined to self-healing through motion. Think of all that is in motion in your physical body now and recognize that all that motion is dedicated to one purpose, to keep you healthy and well. Thus motion is natural healing.

Now you may well ask, "What about the motion of cancer for instance, creating a malignant growth, a growth that is not healthy?" The Law of Motion is constantly in action to create health, but the Law of Motion is subject to human choice in one's own human body as any other aspect of Universal Law. The law is absolute, but all laws interact with the Law of Freedom of Choice. Sometimes a person creates things in their body that are not healthy. The body will still be in motion to try to remove the obstruction, but it is not always successful. The motion does not always act in a healing way, for the human thought pattern may be in opposition to the natural motion of the inner body and thus a cold, flu or various diseases will be the result of the human thought. The Law of Motion is a feeling law. It is also healing in outward activity of the body such as hugging, kissing and caressing. The motion of the tongue, teeth and lips when one is speaking as well as the motion of the larynx and diaphragm, all the inner motions used in the process of speech, require motion to achieve speech. Speech can be very healing. The brain processes thought and the process uses electricity and electricity is always in motion. The neurons of your brain are in constant motion as thought after thought is being processed. The muscle itself moves because of the thought. If the thought is loving, then healing must take place through all the motion of the body. If it is not loving obviously the opposite will result.

Therefore, thought is involved in the Law of Motion as it pertains to healing. If one understood this fully, there would be much more healing and much less disease. Now, humans also are healed by motions that they do not participate in. Let us use a very graphic example. A human may be under anesthesia for a medical procedure, thus the human is not actively participating in the motion made by the medical healing team. Their motions are also guided to healing this patient. All this motion has the same goal, healing. The inner body of the patient may still be in active motion, certainly the heart is beating, the blood is circulating, etc., but the motion of other human beings interacting with the inner body motion of the patient will create healing. Another example of healing through motion is watching nature in action. Sitting quietly in an outdoor place, watching the grass, the trees, the animals such as, squirrels, birds and chipmunks moving and this motion and action crates peace within the individual observing and they are receiving healing. Motion is always there. Nothing ever completely ceases moving. This is why you may hold a mineral such as a crystal in your hand or against a certain part of your body and the body will respond to the healing energy of the crystal. For the atoms of the crystal are still in motion. The crystal may not be capable of independent movement, but the atoms, the healing energy in the mineral are still in action and begin a healing process. Everything animal, plant and mineral, are still in action and begin a healing process. Everything animal, plant and mineral is constantly in motion and motion is directed toward healing. This is the Law of Motion.

24

UNIVERSAL SPIRITUAL LAW OF DISCRETION

The Law of Discretion simply put, means the ability to examine every facet available in a given situation and then in a non-judgmental way choose to do that which will benefit the most people in the best possible way, and to the highest possible degree. It is, however, much broader than that. Discretion is related to judgement, but it is not just judgement, it is a much more evolved aspect of choice than judgement is. Discretion means working fully within the Law of Love and the Law of Attraction, and other laws previously discussed. When one is using discretion, one is never impetuous, one never makes a decision without gaining as much information as possible, one is not critical of other life forms and one does not believe that their choice is the only choice. They simply believe that given a certain set of circumstances it is the best choice that is right for them.

There is a passage that Paul wrote in his letters to his many congregations, "The Gift of Discernment", he called it and he specifically spoke of the discernment of good and evil spirits. Discernment is a vital part of discretion. Discernment means to perceive or recognize things clearly with good judgement. Only by using the power of discernment can you fully use the power of discretion (decision making}. In more simple terms, only by using good judgement and seeing things clearly can you fully use the power of exercising good decision making. You must then operate not only at a physical level in decision making, but at a spiritual level as well. There is a co-relationship of discernment and discretion. One cannot exist without the other. They are co-dependent, but then, all of Universal Law is co-dependent.

Let me use a common example. Two spouses are in disagreement on a very vital portion of their life together. He wishes to do something in a certain way, she wishes to do it in a very different way. They cannot agree. Each of them are convinced that their way is the only way. The arguments become stronger, more frequent, more destructive to the fiber of their matrimonial joy. Neither of them are being discerning, and discretion cannot exist without discernment. She is making no attempt to understand why he wishes to do it in his way. He is making no attempt to understand why she wishes to do it her way. Each is only stubbornly convinced that they shall have the desired result their way. If each of them would stop and do a number of things, examine their real motivation for wishing to do it in a certain way, listen with absolute and concentrated loving attention to what their spouse is wishing to accomplish and not being judgmental, they would eventually, through conversation and compromise arrive at a amicable decision. Thus they would discern (acknowledge and perceive) the others thought pattern. They would then be able to use discretion (understanding) in their actions to the other. She would cease yelling at him and calling him selfish and thoughtless. He would cease yelling at her and calling her a nag, and other less complimentary terms. Discernment, and discretion are both necessary for discretion to work. Discretion is the ability to use information in a valid, productive and positive way. Once all of the information is gathered, then by sifting through it using discernment you are able to arrive at a desirable conclusion.

Discretion is not judgement, it is decision making from an educated basis. Discernment is the gathering of the information and then being able to effectively use it. Discernment, then is a part of the gift of wisdom, and wisdom is a part of the Law of Discretion, they are two valid parts of a single thing. Discerning people and discreet people do not make emotional decisions, they make decisions based on logic and fact.

Emotion is necessary, for emotion is energy. Thus, with the information provided, a discreet conclusion may be reached. When persons are discerning in their choice of friends, they generally will find friends of a lasting nature and friends of a shared kind of consciousness. If they will use the same discernment when a friendship is no longer valid because the consciousness of the individual has changed, there would be fewer angry endings of friendship. Another example; two persons have formed a friendship because they share many mutual interests. They have, through the use of the Law of Discretion come to the conclusion that they have much in common. They have discreetly understood that the other is a potential friend and have embarked on a friendship, but in time they change, the interests are no longer the same. In most cases what happens is, they each try to convince the other to be what they once were, or to be what they now are. This does not work. Under the Law of Discretion they would lovingly admit to one another that their interests are no longer great, their commonality is not as binding and bonding as it once was. They would agree to lovingly each see their own pathway of evolvement, and to always leave the door open to a possible resumption of the friendship. They would not cease to love one another and part as enemies, but rather part as former and possibly future friends. Nations would not come to war if they were more discreet and instead of calling each other enemy and inferior, they would examine the facts and find that there are no enemies and no inferiors, there would be no more war.

The Law of Discretion is a profound and binding law upon all of creation. For creation is discreet, nothing is created that is not needful or valuable. There are no mistakes it creation and everything that exists, exists because under the Law of Discretion it is a needful thing. The Law of Discretion is used in the creation of a new incarnation for each human. The egg and the sperm are exemplary in their use of the Law of Discretion. Only one sperm may impregnate one egg. In the Law of Discretion all other things are set aside, decisions are made, the correct sperm and the correct egg come together and produce the correct incarnate human being. There are no mistakes. The egg does not accept the first sperm or perhaps the first many. Medical science has come to the conclusion that the continuing touching of the sperm against the egg eventually weakens the egg case and the lucky sperm is the next one to touch, this is not so. It is true that the touch of the sperm to egg weakens the egg case but under the Law of Discretion the egg case is weakened for a particular sperm.to unite with that particular egg. There is not random choice involved, and because both the egg and sperm are alive and have consciousness, they know that they are choosing each other and that they are the perfect pairing for that particular human being. Thus, the sperm that is to be mated with the egg would not even consider being the first one, for it could not penetrate the egg case, but rather wait until the proper instant in infinity that it is then able to enter easily, freely, join with the egg and the new incarnation of humanity has now begun. Obviously SCIENCE HAS A LOT TO LEARN ABOUT THE FACT THAT THERE IS NO COINCIDENCE, RANDOMNESS OR ACCIDENTS. The universe is in itself in perfect order and balance. We need to be able to recognize this and use it.

Thus, spirit watches with endless fascination in many life forms, how the Law of Discretion is working. Many spouses occasionally disagree. If one would remember the Law of Discretion, and bring full discernment, both spouses using not only their physical senses, but their spiritual senses to truly understand what the other one is feeling, saying, thinking and doing, the quarrels would be much shorter and much less frequent. In the emotional aspect both discernment and discretion flee, when that happens the distant dark relative of discretion takes over, that is called judgement. Judgement is reasonless, it just exists. Discretion on the other hand, is fully logical, reasonable and correct thought pattern. Look about you, look upon all the life forms that share your home and know that each of them is there because of the Law of Discretion.

Discretion could be defined as thoughtful choice, but unfortunately throughout the universe the life forms are not always using it, but then that is true of everything. Laws of the universe cannot be broken by not being discreet in your dealings. You are not breaking the law, that is impossible. You are making a choice to harm yourself, which is possible.

Discretion also means, in a very human sense, and in a universal sense that you have responsibility to yourself, to certain other life forms that you have chosen to take responsibility for and to the universe in which you live. You will therefore accept these responsibilities, work within them, making the best possible choices. You will also, as a discreet individual not interfere in the life plans and responsibilities of other life forms. For instance, if you now have younger children, who are as yet your responsibility and older grown children who are no longer your responsibility, you must interfere as a discreet parent using discretion in the affairs of your younger children, for they are not yet mature to make their own discreet decisions. In the affairs of the elder children you have no legal obligation to them. Your little children are not yet mature enough, your elder children are, although at times they do not seem to be. This is true of many life forms. You and your spouse under the laws of your community have willingly accepted certain responsibilities to one another. This is good, as long as each for you are discreet in knowing where your responsibility to your spouse begins and where it ends. As long as each of you are following the Law of Discretion where decision making is concerned, you may not make decisions for your spouse, not she for you. Each makes their own personal decision, and together work at decisions that are family decisions.

Discreet, then does not mean secretive, as many people believe. It means personal responsibility, logical thought, use of discernment, using all the spiritual gifts of insight gaining all the information available so that you may with discretion keep your life focused where you wish it to go. It is often said that, "Discretion is the better part of valor". Indeed, valor is too often interpreted to mean being brave, rather it should be thought of as resourceful, reliable and responsible. A person who is practicing discretion will be all of those things and thus will be a brave individual. One of the most difficult things for any person to do is to be absolutely self-responsible. That takes great courage, great maturity and great willingness to not only accept, but never complain about the result of the choices you make. How many people have you met in your lifetime, who never complain and never try to assign at least some of the responsibility to someone else? Obviously, in this day and time it is rare to find people who realize the importance and benefit of taking responsibility for their thoughts, words and deeds.

Helpful Webster's Definitions:

Discretion- examine facts of a situation with sound judgement and making the best decision for all

Discernment- to perceive or recognize clearly

Universal Spiritual Law of Discretion and Healing

The law of Discretion is vast in potential. Discretion is the ability to see things and discern between them, as to whether they are something that you choose to experience or choose not to experience, to put it quite simply. All humans are under and part of the Law of Discretion, but most humans do not know this, believing they are ruled by forces outside of themselves. Discretion would simply say, "I do not choose to be ill, I choose to experience good health". Discretion points the way to achieving good health, for instance, proper thinking, loving thought, proper care in a physical way of the body and, resting it properly, giving it goals to achieve and having enthusiasm for life. Discreet activity is not hidden, it is open for those who use discretion in their planning, find that after thinking about something for a period of time, meditating and praying, it no longer seems something they chose or it may become even more valuable. The greater the value of choice made with discretion, the greater the healing energy. It does not take discretion to perceive when a child is not feeling well, but discretion on the part of the parent is necessary to decide what measures to take to heal the child. Thus the very Law of Discretion begins the act of healing in concert with all of the other laws.

Saint Paul spoke of discretion of good and evil spirits as one of the gifts for the holy spirit and it is, for there is a difference between good and evil. But we are not talking of discarnate spirit, we are talking of the spirit of every life form. There is discretion, one's own spirit is the object of one' s discretion, one must know within one's self that they are basically divine and loving. They must use discernment to find this out. They must be willing to except the truth of their own individual self. This the real meaning of discretion between good and evil. Evil is live spelled backwards. Those who are called evil for any reason, are those who have not yet learned how to live in a more loving, giving, sharing and receiving fashion. THAT IS WHAT EVIL AND IGNORANCE TRULY IS, LACK OF KNOWLEDGE OR MISUSE OF KNOWLEDGE. Wisdom is using knowledge correctly. There is discernment in a decision made from knowledge gathered. Wisdom is correct usage. Knowledge, without wisdom, can lead to incorrect usage. Therefore, discerning of our thought patterns through meditation and discerning of what we believe ourselves to be, is vital to healing. If discernment brings the conclusion that the person wants to be healed, the healing will begin. If consciously or not consciously, discernment brings the decision that healing is not the choice, then healing will not occur or if healing of one particular thing may happen, but that does not mean that health will be maintained, for the desire to be healthy must be a constant thing. It must be nourished every day. Those then who discern between their own good and evil thoughts,(thought forms of ignorance),are able to think more lovingly and truthfully and as it is practiced over a period of time, the incidence of less than loving thought, becomes fewer and fewer until Christhood is achieved. Discernment is vital to health. Discernment brings healing, when healing is what is discerned to be the choice of the individual.

25

APPLICATION OF UNIVERSAL SPIRITUAL LAWS

Now let us move to the application of Universal Laws. This is the part that is challenging, rewarding and difficult. There are no humans that fully understand Universal Law. Therefore, we must be content, not with understanding fully Universal Law, but with working to the best of our ability within the law. These laws exist for your betterment, for the progression of your soul's yearning, for the enrichment of your life physically and spiritually. The use then of Universal Law is possible, even without totally understanding it, in the same way that an individual may flick a light switch and use the switch, even if that individual has no understanding of electricity or of why the light goes on. Using Universal Law is not difficult, but it requires a great willingness upon the part of each individual to take upon themselves the desire to basically interact with every life form in the most loving, useful and harmonious way that it is possible for them to do. It requires that a person wants very much to enrich their life, to grow and evolve spiritually, to achieve peace and comfort in their physical existence and to express themselves creatively in whatever ways they are capable of doing. Also, to share themselves with others to the extent of their abilities to do so and to find the things in their life that will give them the greatest sense of pleasure, joy and accomplishment.

All Universal law leads towards pleasure and joy and the laws actually leads back into itself. The only thing that you need to keep in mind is that Universal Law is self-perpetuating, eternal, infinite and that each individual is acting in accordance with the law when they are acting in loving ways, and that means loving toward every other life form. For example, it is not a loving act to deliberately step upon a caterpillar, but to observe the characteristics of that life form and to admire the beauty is a loving act. When one is trying to live according to the Law of Love, they will automatically be observing, to the extent of their own progression, all of the other laws, and this is the great point that one must remember, the primacy of the Law of Love. Each time you act, speak and think in loving ways, all other laws are also being observed. It is impossible not to follow Universal Law, even acting in what may seem to be unloving, destructive fashion does not break Universal Law. You are simply not observing it. The law cannot be broken, it can be deliberately unobserved, but because one person is unloving does not mean that the law ceases to exist. It simply means that that person has not yet learned that they will be happier, more productive, have a more peaceful, harmonious, joyous and contented experience if they permit themselves to love.

Everything that occurs, no matter whether it is positive or unloving and destructive, is in observance of or goes in accordance to Universal Laws. When one does this in a loving fashion they are doing it in a more spiritually progressive manner. Doing any evil is also in conjunction with Universal Laws because it governs everything that happens. However a negative, harmful or evil observance or act brings like results to the one who creates them and thus slows their progression and makes their self-selected lessons far more difficult for themselves. So one cannot escape Universal Law. One has no choice but to be governed by it. However they do have a choice in how they live by the laws and that is in a positive or negative way. Let us go back to the situation in Germany of WWII. In and of itself, taken as an isolated activity, could not totally happen again. It cannot because the law is supreme, out of these acts reformation, the shifting of consciousness of humans, an increased respect of life came as a decision to allow the most persecuted of the non-acceptable individuals to have a homeland of their own that other nations agreed to help them protect. Israel is a direct result of the activities of that particular group of people, the very thing they least desire to have happen did happen, thus the Law of Love was still the final decision maker, it cannot be broken. People may act in unloving ways, but still the law is unbroken. To understand Universal Law one must understand love. This is the difference between Universal Law and man-made laws which do not have love as their total basis or often even partial basis.

In summary the information, wisdom, truth and insights presented in love and with a desire to help everyone who, at their individual stage in life and spiritual evolvement, desire specific guidelines that will help them prepare to move into the new millennium. This new age is a reality and not just a name and we will all make our own decision as to our fate or place in the new enlightened order of life. As so often stressed in this book, LOVE will be the entire basis for the new thinking lifestyle. This will not be an easy transition for many people now on this earth since many societies have never been taught or simply slowly moved away, though life's experiences, from a positive, loving and Golden Rule basis for their thoughts, words and deeds.

As indicated in the Universal Laws, we always have a choice and the true inner spirit of all creation is a loving part of God. But with the increasing challenges of life we all face and have created, the basis and heart of the existence has been forgotten or intentionally misrepresented or simply hidden. This is what happens when the

Universal Laws are not known or used to their fullest. The human nature, emotions, ego, ignorance and laziness easily gets between our unnatural physical existence and our true inner spiritual essence. That is easy to do, since on this earth we live in a physical plane of existence. So many humans go by the saying "When in Rome, do as the Romans do" and don't look within themselves for the truth and wisdom that is available to all of us.

We often put our faith and belief in others that are always willing to serve in a position of authority, power and control. It often seems like the easy way and avoids taking responsibility for one's self and making the effort to do your own work and growth yourself. This never works in the long run. The invaluable insights presented in this book helps all who seek to find the answer and for those who ask to receive. No one has to find God or the Oneness of Creation through anyone else since WE ARE ALL A PART OF IT AND IT IS WITHIN ALL OF US. Others can only assist and advise us. We must do the work ourselves and understand that we create our own life's path which, of course, interacts with those we come in contact with.

If one truly studies the Universal Laws, they will realize that no one or nothing is placed above anything else. How can it be if IT (creation) is One and everything that exists is simply an individualization of the One True God. No matter what name you want to give it, it doesn't change what it truly is and that is LOVE in physical and spiritual existence and expression.

The Universal Laws were not made or created. Instead the Universal Laws simply were and they created the universe, they are not amendable. They govern all things so it doesn't take much thinking or intelligence to figure out the great wisdom and power in understanding them and applying them in a positive loving way to one's own thoughts, words, deeds and beliefs. This allows one to create the life they choose. It is very important to understand that Universal Laws apply to all levels of consciousness from the lowest to the highest level of spiritual consciousness. Remember we all function on a number of levels of consciousness and most of us are only consciously aware of the lower physical levels. So our higher and lower levels of consciousness are helping direct our life and evolution. That is why all things that happen in our life, we wonder where it came from and we immediately try to find someone else to take the blame or responsibility.

Thus, when we don't take responsibility and learn the appropriate growth lessons, we find ourselves having to repeat the lesson. Think about it, most people don't like to repeat lessons. So study, learn and understand the Universal Laws so you can use them to advance your spiritual growth and evolution and minimize the number of times you have to be faced with a challenging lesson, before you learn it.

There are many Universal Laws, but this book has presented the primary law, the secondary laws and some of the tertiary laws. We need to open our minds, look deep within ourselves and objectively study and acquaint ourselves with our true essence which is spiritual. We need to realize that we are here on this earth to learn lessons to assist our spiritual growth. Thus knowing the rules, (Universal Spiritual Laws) makes our evolutionary path shorter and easier and helps fill it with joy. More and more people are awaking spiritually and this book can be an important stepping stone in anyone's spiritual evolvement and I offer it to anyone with love that opens themselves to spiritual wisdom and guidance.

26

COMMENTS ON MEDICAL SCIENCE HEALING

The major purpose for this book on Universal Spiritual Laws has already been commented on, is to present the true laws that govern both physical and spiritual life. So now we can say that "ignorance of law is not an excuse". As stated, these are truly unbreakable laws. You will always be governed by them and your thoughts, words and deeds will determine whether they have a positive effect on your life or they make your life more challenging.

I wanted to include a brief insight as to how each law relates to healing for the two rather obvious reasons: first, I have spent a major part of my life first learning about healing both medically and spiritually and secondly, both medical and spiritual healing has a profound effect on your quality of life as well as your spiritual evolvement, which is why we are on this physical planet.

I would like to give you some of the insights to healing I have gained over the last approximately fifty years from close observation in my medical practice as well as my study and research into spirituality. My scientific background (engineering, etc.) has caused me to approach my research from a questioning standpoint. I want to first say, as I have always said in all of my writing and public speaking, that during my entire practice of medicine I always adhered to the standard accepted principles of the medical profession. However, as an OB/GYN, I had the advantage of more flexibility with my patients, since many of them, particularly the obstetrical patients were seeing me for normal, natural and healthy conditions.

I will go into more detail about healing in my next book, but want to give you some general insights in this book. There is no doubt that medical science as it continues to develop, is invaluable to our physical healing. But remember, like everything else, medical science is ever changing (Law of Change). I draw your attention to the fact that alternative medicine has gained far more credibility and application since I started in practice in 1981. I can assure you, there is far more to learn about healing and it will occur in due time.

I feel and predict that the biggest change that needs to be made, is to focus more on the thinking, beliefs, life experiences and situations of the patient. So by "looking" within the patient to get insights into how the above actions of the patient has contributed to the health condition of the patient. Then by changing the thinking, beliefs and life situation of the patient, thereby helping the patient, "let go" of the condition. Certainly, the use of medical techniques can in ways help facilitate the cure. The healing aspects of the Universal Spiritual Laws give insights to how the factors creating the health condition were created and how they can be changed to eliminate the condition.

Of course, in order to really get to the real techniques of healing, many of the aspects and beliefs that have been preached and taught over thousands of years will need to be dispelled and changed in order to fully understand the ultimate basis of illness and disease. The true origins come from within the patient and not from outside the patient. Changing patients and physician's thinking and beliefs will certainly take time, but can be done as healers are willing to investigate and open to new thinking. It is slowly beginning even now. Many of the healing techniques are known even now, but are not widely understood or accepted. Remember the biblical saying, "Physician heal thyself". There are many historical and biblical accounts of hands-on healing without medicines or surgery. I don't remember hearing any biblical accounts of Jesus or other historical healers carrying a black doctors bag to help them with their healings.

I have seen many examples in my medical practice of patient responses or action that are not supposed to occur. General examples of this are newborn babies doing things that are not expected by medical science or principles, but their actions support my beliefs that there is far more to a newborn than classically attributed to them. The same has occurred with obstetrical patients or patients desiring pregnancy.

The more frequent area of my practice where I witnessed unexpected occurrences was with my gynecological patients. In general, it was not uncommon to have a patient with significant symptoms (pain, etc.) and then at the time of surgery there was no physical evidence of anything that would explain the symptoms. However after the surgery, the patients' symptoms were gone. One specific case I learned a great deal from with respect to healing very significant long term pain without medication or surgery, is one that I will never forget. I was able to eliminate the severe pain by simply talking and listening to the patient. I don't feel I actually cured her of anything, I simply, by listening to her, was able to give her the keys and insights to her problem that helped change her beliefs and thinking, which allowed her to heal herself. It was quite amazing to see this happen. All that caused this can be easily explained by Universal Laws first being used in a negative way and then applying them in a positive way. Witnessing these things happen, lends great credibility to the validity and truthfulness of the Universal Spiritual Laws as given in this book.

So for a considerable amount of time there will be a need of evolving medical science and techniques, but by being willing to open physician's and patient's minds and be willing to consider, research into the non-physical aspects of healing, we will make great progress in truly healing all illness and disease. The non-physical or spiritual healing techniques will slowly replace the physical or mechanical techniques as more and more physicians, researchers and patients see the results that can be achieved as I have. Over thousands of years we have created illness and disease and hopefully we can eliminate them in a much shorter time. Just think of the rapid technological advances that have occurred on this earth in the last 260 years since the start of the Industrial Revolution in about 1760. The advances since then have been somewhat exponential not linear. So change and evolution are speeding up and will continue to do so in the future. This has been well demonstrated in the medical profession as well as in many areas of our life.

So open your mind, look within yourself, study the Universal Spiritual Laws and apply them to your life and help make the needed changes to make this a better world. In my next book I will present numerous aspects of life that many people, particularly in the Western World, have not been exposed to or taught, often for self-serving reasons, that will help better understand the real truths of life in both the physical as well as the spiritual realm. I have spent many years being taught these truths as a researcher and a physician and I feel my main purpose in this life is to make this valuable truth available to those who are also seekers of the Light and Truth. What you decide to believe and do with the information is totally up to you. I feel what I have been taught is very logical and makes more sense about life than many other beliefs and I have found it the most fascinating study and research I have done. So I give you this information in Love and Light and hope you enjoy it and benefit from it as I have.

INDEX LISTING OF UNIVERSAL SPIRITUAL LAWS

1. The Law of Love states that every aspect of the Consciousness of God and creation loves itself and every other aspect of God unconditionally. It is the basis for all other Universal Spiritual Laws (USL).

2. The Law of Attraction states that what any aspect of the Consciousness of God sends forth in thought form will return to itself. What you give returns to you or you reap what you sow. It gives the right for thoughts to attract necessary elements to create.

3. The Law of Cause and Effect states that for everything that happens there is a cause. That which is done produces an effect. Every action has an equal and opposite reaction.

4. The Law of Freedom of Choice states that in every life form, limitless choice is always available. With this freedom goes absolute responsibility for the choices that are made.

5. The Law of Responsibility states that aspects and life forms of the Universal Consciousness are responsible for everything they think, say and do and must expect the consequences of them.

6. The Law of Abundance states that there is absolute, total, unending and infinite abundance in the universe and every aspect of the Consciousness of God may

receive any degree of abundance they choose to receive. It is the mind that creates abundance.

7. The law of Harmony states that all things in the universe are in absolute harmony with all other things. Nothing may be out of harmony even if to human sensitivity it seems to be.

8. The Law of Vibration states that each and every aspect of creation vibrates at its own perfect level. Vibration is action and everything is always in action and it is in action perfectly with every other aspect of the Consciousness of God.

9. The Law of Forgiveness states that forgiveness means to extend to every other aspect of the Consciousness of God and self, total love and to understand and allow to become unimportant that which has happened which may have caused distress.

10. The Law of Karma is a system of checks and balances. It provides a person with the opportunity to rectify that which has been inappropriately or improperly handled at any time in the past. Karma is an aspect of love that is wholly positive. Karma provides a memory pattern that can be balanced by love and forgiveness, not retribution. Balance will occur.

11. The Law of Multiplication states that all things physical and non-physical multiply, nothing is static. All aspects of the universe must multiply, must continue to grow and must reproduce itself. Everything is an active growth pattern.

12. The Law of Attunement states that without things being aware of and attuned to one another, they would "fall apart." It is an

active law that keeps everything where it belongs, doing what it should and tuned to every other thing.

13. The Law of Joy states that because all things are already perfect, constantly multiplying and life is an infinite thing, joy is the natural character of creation. All aspects of God (you, etc) should know nothing but joy at all times.

14. The Law of Need states that nothing in the universe exists unless it is needed. The law is powerful creation in action, bringing to the universe a constant state of creativity for the constant needs of the universe. Need is the basic emotion and structure of creation.

15. The Law of Change keeps all of the action moving in a constantly creative direction. Change is not random, and is for the better. It is the one constant and continuous thing. Change is the essence of any life and any possibility. Without change, possibility does not exist.

16. The Law of Essence states that all things have a central point of being, called essence. The law holds all things, beings and creation into itself with self-awareness. The essence of all things is called Love or God and is the purest form or beginning of everything.

17. The Law of Truth is that there is only truth. Truth is the portion of the substance that holds all of the universe together. The underlying truth of the universe is the "Cosmic Equation": God is One, One is All, All is God. Truth is unchanging

in its being, but it is growing and evolving. There is a great difference between universal truth and human truth.

18. The Law of Purity states that essentially everything that exist is pure within itself since all that exist is God, and God could not be other than pure. It states God is All and All is God.

19. The Law of Balance states that each and every aspect of the Consciousness of God must be in balance with every other aspect. No aspect of God is more important than any other aspect. All are in balance to one another and balance is that perfect point keeping the physical universe in perfect order.

20. The Law of Patience states that all things are created in the exact perfect length of time required for their perfect creation. Patience is creation in action and creates more.

21. The Law of creation states that "I am, therefore I create". It is more than just making something, it is a major part of self-awareness. Creation starts with thought and is thought in action. Love, in its infinite state is infinitely creative.

22. The Laws of Prayer, Meditation and Thought will insure that all individuals would have a greater ability to work fully within all of the laws. Prayer (asking, affirming and giving thanks) is the most powerful thought form and is an act of creation. The Law of Meditation states you must receive answers to your questions and with thoughts you create.

23. The Law of Motion states that which moves is constantly creating. Nothing is ever at rest. Without motion nothing

would happen and nothing can cause motion to cease. The Law of Love creates motion.

24. The Law of Discretion means the ability to examine every facet available in any given situation and then in a non-judgmental way to choose to do that which will benefit the most people in the best possible way and to the highest degree. Discernment is a vital part of discretion meaning to perceive or recognize things clearly with good judgement.

ABOUT THE AUTHOR

 Ronald L. Cole, M.D. went from Civil Engineer to Obstetrician/Gynecologist to birth advocate (under water birth in the hospital) and longtime Spiritual researcher and author. Early on he was a co-founder of the Spina Bifida Associate of America. His detailed scientific research into the spiritual aspects of life has extended over 50 years. He realized that knowledge and teaching from mankind's physical side of life mostly comes from a self-serving, false and prejudicial basis. Real truth by-passes that and comes from highly evolved spiritual entities in the everlasting or spiritual side of life when he learned about channeling.

This started a 20-year working relationship with Rev. Beverly Burdick-Carey, the most highly evolved medium he worked with. In turn this started a 20 year relationship with a very highly known and evolved spiritual entity, Quan Yin (see book cover), that resulted in this book and well over 500 audio tapes covering most aspects of life. His scientific research has been evaluated by many other sources, logic, consistency over years and applying what he had learned to his personal life and medical practice convinced him of the research's validity.

He simply asked you to keep an open mind.

Dr. Cole has been featured in numerous newspaper and magazine articles and appeared on radio and television shows in Houston, Texas and around the country. He has presented at many conferences and meetings and produced three educational birthing videos and a subliminal tape for enlightenment and growth.

Dr. Cole's life has involved many challenging and fun experiences and activities. He played a number of high school and college sports and earned numerous college academic scholarships and awards. He served as an officer in the U.S. Army. He enjoyed numerous other sports including snow and barefoot water skiing, scuba diving up close and personal with humpback whales, whale sharks and manatees and motorcycle riding. He also enjoyed photography and artwork and travel, including a photo safari to Africa. He organized and participated in an official world record sky dive and he owned a recreational ranch in Texas.

Dr. Cole was a past president of the Houston Spina Bifida Association and aided in research of plastic orthopedic braces. As an Obstetrician, he became a birth advocate and performed underwater births and infant massage classes in the hospital. Dr. Cole is now retired from practice and lives with his wife,Karen, and works full time on his writing in Florida.

POSTSCRIPT TO YOU THE READER

I assume you have read the book, so I would like to now make a number of comments and suggestions to you based on my background and the creation of this book. My approximately fifty years of spiritual study was a very thoughtful and objective "scientific" study (civil engineer and medical careers), not just believing what people or books said. My interest, knowledge and understanding evolved over the years as the pure logic, truth, value and wisdom was demonstrated to me as a result of study, research and application during my life and professional careers. I was no different than most of you in that I was given this valuable wisdom and truths as I am now giving it to you.

I understand that the material is quite different than that taught to us as our guidelines and rules of life that were created by previous and current mankind and religious groups. I also know from my own introduction to Universal Spiritual Laws (USL) that much of them are very logical and other parts are somewhat mystifying and somewhat hard to understand. My advice to you is to not worry about that, but to simply give some very open-minded and logical thought to the USL and read all or parts of the book again. I say that because I have obviously read the material I was given numerous times as the book was "written" or transcribed and each time I would read the definitions of the USL, I was better able to see and understand the truth and logic of them. It also helped me understand why mankind "lead us down the path" that would best benefit the ruling class. That is mankind for you. Just look at the situation the world is in today.

Since your family, friends, life and our world can greatly benefit from knowing and living by USL, it is worth reviewing the knowledge again and discussing it with your family and/or whoever you feel comfortable talking to about these USL and their applications. Since it was obvious USL would allow us to create "new" and truthful beliefs and understandings of our physical and spiritual lives, I spent considerable time helping make USL available to anyone interested in advancing their physical and spiritual evolvement and creating the perfect and loving world God originally created for us. I hope this book serves you well. Simply start with small steps, and remember, it is your choice.

Printed in the United States
By Bookmasters